ALI KAZIM

SUSPENDED IN TIME

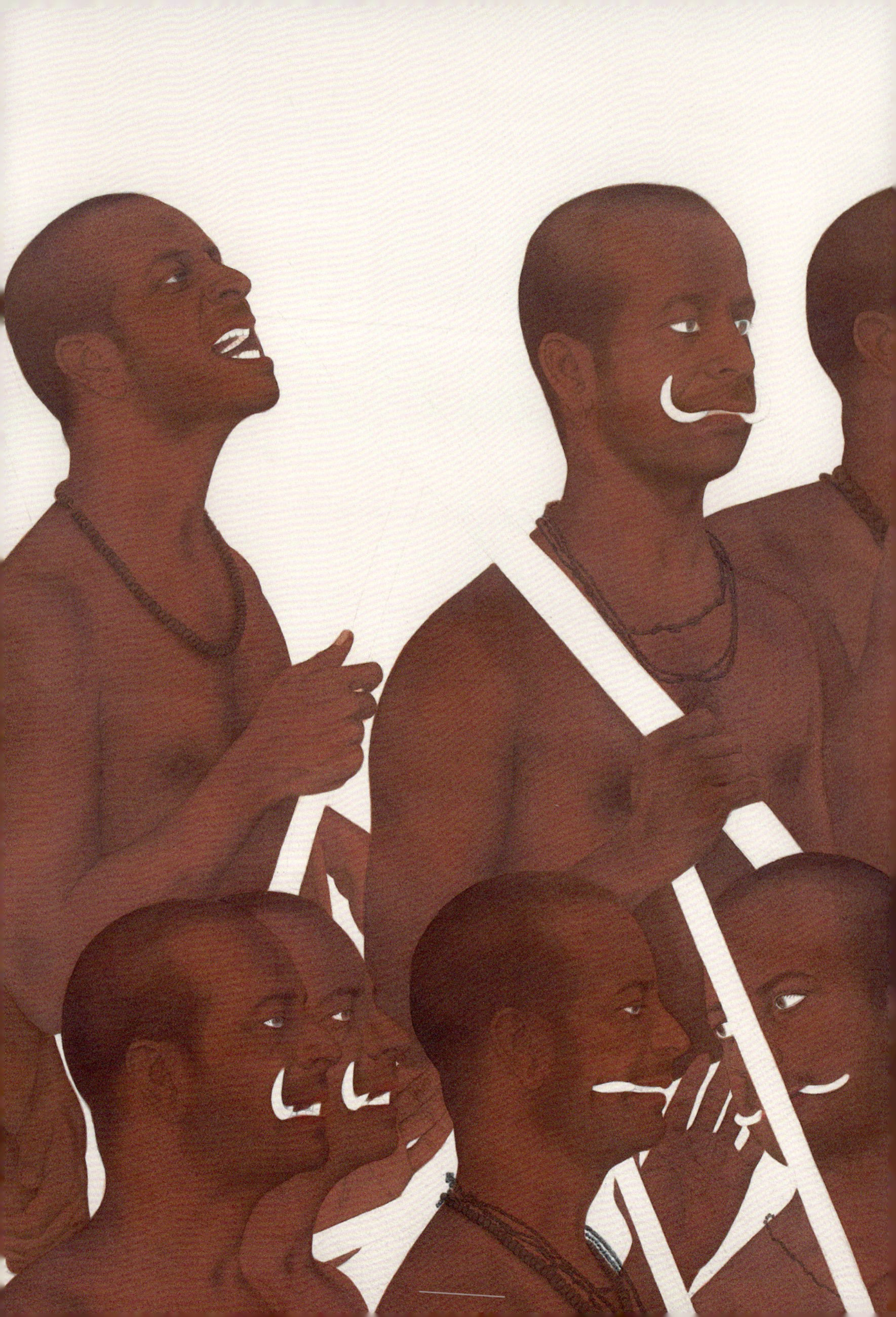

ALI KAZIM

SUSPENDED IN TIME

Mallica Kumbera Landrus

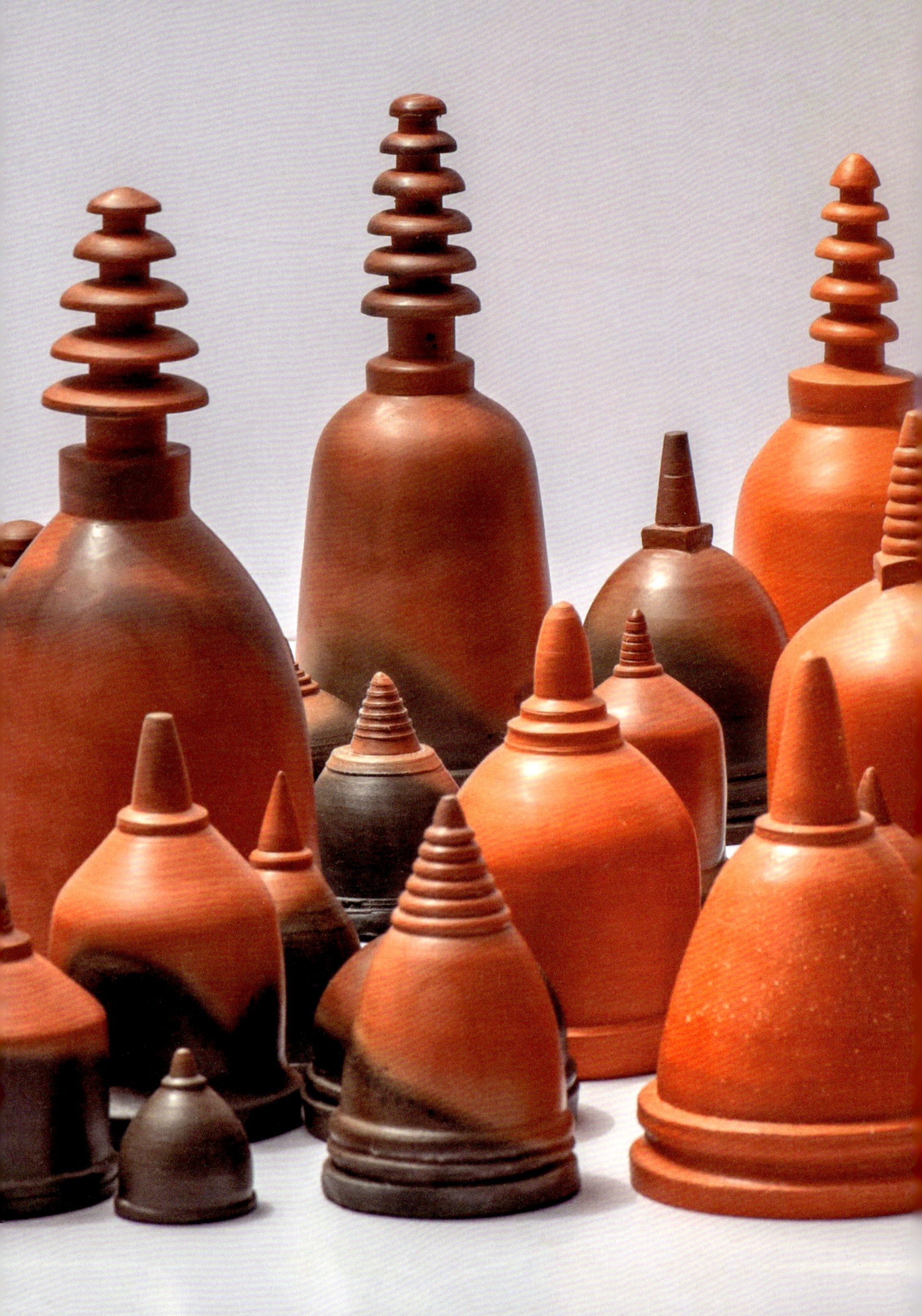

CONTENTS

FOREWORD

ALI KAZIM, ONE OF THE most exciting contemporary artists working in Pakistan today, has spoken about how objects from the distant past can act as 'time-travelling keys'. How a small clay sculpture or a fingerprint on a pottery sherd can connect us, directly and viscerally, to the people who originally made and used them. *Ali Kazim: Suspended in Time* is a solo exhibition informed by the time he spent with these time-travelling keys in the Ashmolean. During a residency here in 2019 we opened the Museum's South Asian collections to Kazim, who spent days browsing through the stores and galleries, and examining objects up close in the study rooms. Kazim's engagement with the material and visual traditions of the subcontinent encourages us in turn to reflect on continuities and breaks; on the timeless and the transient; on how the past informs and influences the present. It is fitting that this exhibition coincides with the 75th anniversary of Pakistan's creation.

An album of Mughal paintings, a small stone image of Ganesha, and other gifts from the subcontinent were presented to the University of Oxford as early as c.1640, decades before the Ashmolean was founded in 1683. The Museum recorded its first acquisition of a major sculpture from the subcontinent in 1686. Today the Ashmolean has a distinguished collection of objects from South Asia, the most comprehensive of its kind after the British Museum and the V&A, and the largest and most prominent of any university museum in the world. However, despite the long history between the subcontinent and Oxford, Kazim is the Ashmolean's first South Asian artist-in-residence.

My heartfelt thanks to Dr Mallica Kumbera Landrus, Keeper of Eastern Art, who discussed and explored the collections in her care with Kazim during his residency, and has curated this exhibition and worked on this catalogue. Presenting Kazim's work in this way would not have been possible without the Elie Khouri Art Foundation, who led the support for this publication. I also wish to thank the Charles Wallace Pakistan Trust for their funding of the artist's travel and accommodation for the exhibition. And I am especially grateful for the generous support of the Kamini and Vindi Banga Family Trust, Tia Fine Art Limited, Ben Brown, Rosamond Brown, the ZVM Rangoonwala Foundation, Tarun and Tarana Sawhney, Tarika and Zafar Ahmadullah, and other benefactors who wish to remain anonymous. I also extend my gratitude to Taimur Hassan, Tarika and Zafar Ahmadullah, Sanda Lwin and Farhad Karim, who graciously parted with works for this exhibition. Special thanks to Amrita Jhaveri from Jhaveri Contemporary for all the help, time and energy she has dedicated to this exhibition.

Above all, my thanks to Ali Kazim for his engagement and involvement with the Museum, and for all his resulting work. It is a pleasure and privilege to be able to share it with our audiences.

Xa Sturgis
Director, Ashmolean Museum.
Fellow, Worcester College, Oxford.

ACKNOWLEDGEMENTS

AS A UNIVERSITY MUSEUM we are grateful to the friends and colleagues who help us display and develop significant contributions in the history of art and visual culture. These contributions help us improve our traditional approaches to – for example – the absence of South Asian contemporary artists at the Ashmolean. We are therefore fortunate to have this opportunity to show the extraordinarily fine and informative work of artist Ali Kazim, who was born in Pakistan and is based in Lahore.

My utmost appreciation goes to Kazim for developing such thoughtful and beautiful work specifically for this exhibition, and for trusting me to curate his art. I benefited greatly from his enthusiasm, generosity, time and valuable support throughout this project. This exhibition is the fruit of a partnership between Kazim and the University of Oxford that began in 2019 with his residency and conversations in the Ashmolean's Department of Eastern Art and the Classical Art Research Centre's Gandhara Connections project.

My sincere thanks to all of the other contributors in this publication – Faisal Devji, Tim Hitchens, Nishant Kumar, Francesca Leoni, Chaitanya Sambrani, Peter Stewart, Emilia Terracciano and Lauren Winch – who shared their knowledge and time to make this catalogue an informative, interdisciplinary resource.

I am grateful to my colleagues in the Ashmolean who were involved in the production of this catalogue, in particular Xa Sturgis, the Director, for his early support of the exhibition, and Declan McCarthy, Head of Publishing and Licensing, who oversaw this publication.

I would like to thank Benjamin Heller, Senior Development Executive, and Agnes Valencak, Head of Exhibitions, who provided invaluable support with various arrangements and plans for the show, and worked so hard to make this publication and exhibition happen. Special thanks also to Clare Flynn for collaborating on the design of the exhibition.

My gratitude also goes to Ally Greathead, Alex Baldwin, Dave Orwell, Kevin Jacques and Tim Crowley for their exceptional work in preparing the objects for display in the exhibition. I also wish to thank our Bodleian colleagues for their support with loans, specifically Alasdair Watson, Gillian Evison, Madeline Slaven, Sallyanne Gilchrist and Ellen Hausner. I am so grateful to the Ashmolean's Marketing Manager Theresa Nicolson and Senior Designer Greg Jones, as well as to Claire Parris and her team in the Press Office, to Balwinder Meyrick in the Finance Office and our Registrar Aisha Burtenshaw.

Special thanks to all my colleagues in the Department of Eastern Art: Alessandra Cereda, Ben Skarratt, Clare Pollard, Dorothy Armstrong, Francesca Leoni, Marie Sinclair, Marwa Ahmed, Sarah Mitchell, Sarah Thorn, and Shelagh Vainker, who know only too well how much I have relied on them.

Mallica Kumbera Landrus
Keeper of Eastern Art, Ashmolean Museum.
Fellow, St Cross College, Oxford.

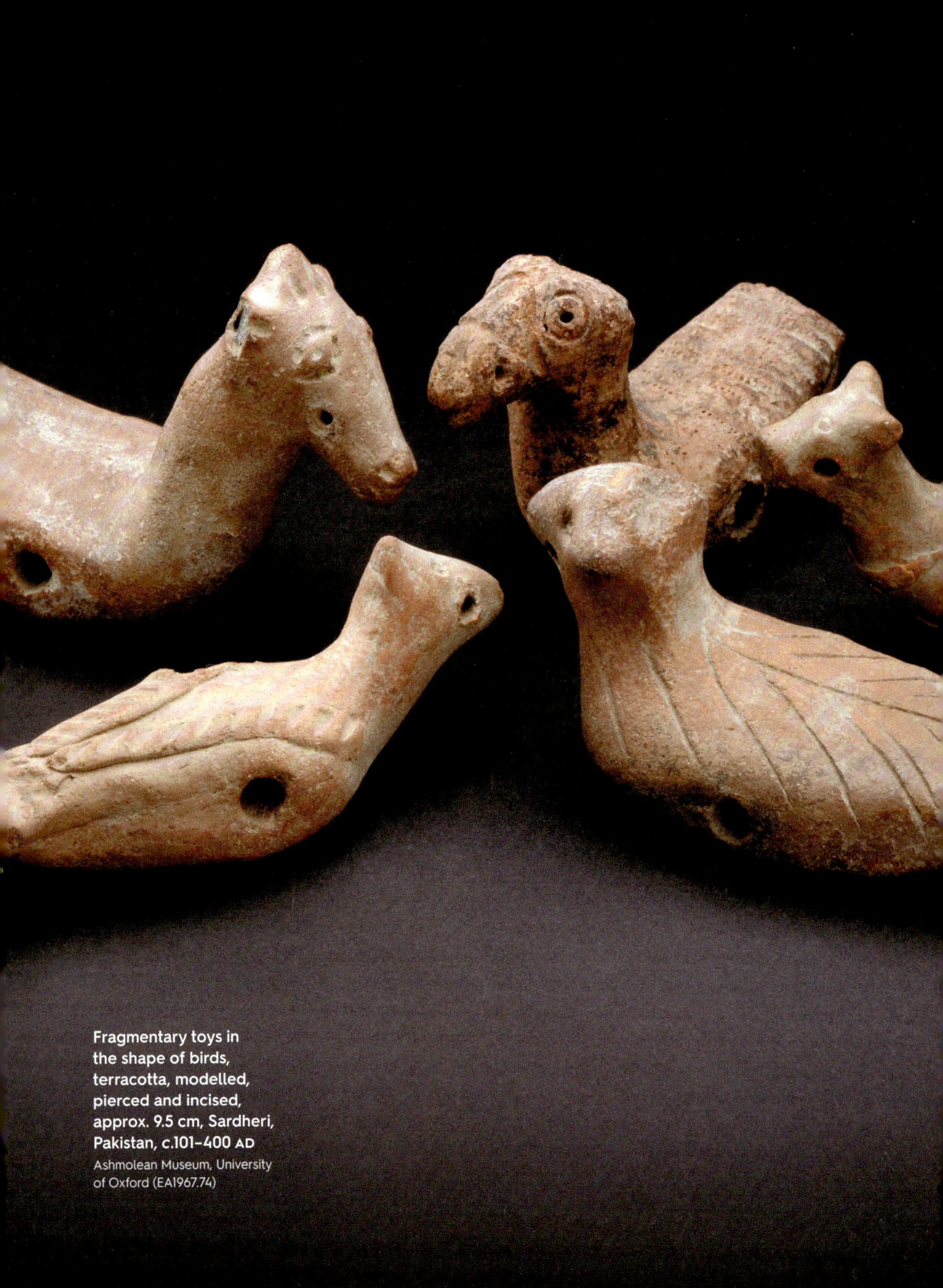

Fragmentary toys in the shape of birds, terracotta, modelled, pierced and incised, approx. 9.5 cm, Sardheri, Pakistan, c.101–400 AD

Ashmolean Museum, University of Oxford (EA1967.74)

IN CONVERSATION WITH ALI KAZIM

In June 2021, Ali Kazim spoke with Mallica Kumbera Landrus about his experiences, his work and the exhibition. The conversations were in Urdu, Hindi and English. The following text is an extract from several conversations, translated from Urdu and Hindi by Mallica Kumbera Landrus.

Mallica Kumbera Landrus: This exhibition focuses mainly on works completed after your residency in the Ashmolean. Could you share your thoughts and experiences about the residency?

Ali Kazim: The ability to see works closely, touch and hold them, was an exceptional opportunity. The residency was specifically to view the Gandharan objects, and I had access to Mughal and Company paintings too. I had seen the Impey birds before, but during the residency I was able to study them unframed, up close, from every angle. Also, one of the most amazing moments was to find the Hudhud, or Hoopoe, in terracotta. Holding these small terracotta birds from the early centuries CE subconsciously resonated with me. Several months later when I started to prepare for the Lahore Biennale 2020, I made clay birds for *The Conference of Birds* installation. The trigger was certainly the terracotta birds I had seen in the Ashmolean. To now be part of a show with works I have admired, and observed closely, is a privilege.

MKL: Let's go back to the beginning. What is an early memory of your interest in art?

AK: My earliest memory is at age three, when I joined older children in a primary school, drawing pictures. The teacher praised my drawing of a mango as exceptional. Being appreciated by that teacher helped me think that this was something I could do well. In later years, before special events I would help with decorating the school by drawing pictures on the walls. I realised early that I stood out in my school, because no one else could draw like me.

MKL: How important do you think it was, for your work, that you started life in your village?

AK: My village, Pattoki, is a two-hour drive from Lahore. A further 90 minutes takes you to the Harappan archaeological site, which I rarely visited as a child. I had many questions about picture making, which led my primary school teacher to suggest that I speak to the cinema board painters in town. I approached the billboard painters and eventually learnt much from them. Later, when I saw Dilip Kumar sculpting in a movie, I approached furniture makers to learn the fundamentals of carving wood. Similarly, I watched another actor shaping a pot, and went to the other side of my village to learn from potters there. Curiosity, a desire to learn, and a case of 'life imitating film' guided me towards particular individuals. My *ustad* (expert) among the cinema board painters was the first person to mention the National College of Arts (NCA) in Lahore. While he steered me to finish my higher secondary education, I helped him paint portraits of circus and carnival people, as well as hoardings and billboards. After I finished my secondary exams, I travelled with him and a circus caravan to various towns.

MKL: What did your parents think of your interests?

AK: My peers in school were often in trouble. My parents were relieved that I was interested in art and not in bad company. However, I did not know what subjects to study. Some people advised my family to rein me in and suggested nursing and medicine. I was around 15 years old when I arrived in the city of Kasur for a one-year diploma in nursing. This was perhaps the start of my practical life. While studying to become a nurse, my mind was always on art and the NCA, but I did not know how I was going to get there.

MKL: So how did you finally reach the NCA?

AK: I drew a portrait of a doctor in Kasur. When I finished my diploma, he offered to recommend me for work at the Gulab Devi Chest Hospital in Lahore. In addition, he also offered evening work in his own clinic. This opportunity - to work in the largest chest hospital in Punjab and in a private clinic - was exciting for me only because it would take me to Lahore and closer to the NCA.

When I arrived in Lahore, I knew the address of the NCA but I lacked the confidence to enter its gates and speak to people. I had read about Pak Tea House in Anarkali, an old bazaar in Lahore. This was where progressive writers had gathered in the past, a place of intimate literary gatherings, and performances of music, dance and poetry. However, the romantic era that I had read about was from the 1970s; in the 1990s it was a very different place. Walking around Anarkali one day, I came across someone painting a cityscape. After waiting for him to finish, when he was packing up his easel, I explained my interest in the NCA. The artist was a Punjab University student, and he invited me to visit him with my portfolio. Soon, I started freehand drawing under his guidance.

Meanwhile, my work as a nurse continued. From 7am to 2pm I was in the hospital; from 3pm to 5pm I worked on my drawings, and from 5pm to 9pm I was working at the doctor's clinic. After 9pm, I would take my work to show the student artist. I repeated this routine for a whole year.

MKL: How have your experiences as a nurse influenced your work today?
AK: The right tools, in the right place, are important elements of discipline in hospital work. Looking closely at the human body; cutting, opening and stitching parts of it also contributed to my continued interests in drawing the body and portraits. My work on the *Ruins* series took years to prepare, and discipline certainly played a role there.
MKL: How did the NCA contribute to or change your way of thinking?
AK: The NCA contrasted greatly with my background. In the early days, I was hesitant and felt alone, but eventually I realised students were judged only for their work. Discussions at the end of each day were based around that - not on one's background.
MKL: How and when did you start thinking of the Slade School in London?
AK: As several NCA faculty members were Slade alumni, the Slade was well known at the NCA. Around 2004 I applied for the ROSL (Royal Over-Seas League) travel scholarship. The following year, I gathered my 10–15 finished works in a portfolio and travelled to the UK. For the next few years I returned as a visitor, eventually joining the Slade in 2009.
MKL: Was there a huge difference between your life at the NCA and the Slade?
AK: While at the NCA, I had to work hard to save money for tuition. I taught drawing, and during the weekends painted portraits and landscapes on commission. It was a struggle to survive. When I graduated and started to exhibit, money started to trickle in. By 2009 I had saved enough to either buy a house or pursue further studies. I chose to spend the funds on my education.

For two years at the Slade, I really enjoyed my student life. Students came from across the world and brought their own cultural ways of working. I did not actively seek to learn some of their ways, but realised much later that I had picked up some ways of working from them.
MKL: Would you say something about how your experiences led to new ideas?
AK: In my earlier works, whether organic forms or portraits, I was interested in the materiality of the work. At the Slade I worked on leather, skin, body and bodily material such as human hair. I was fascinated by the material and the loaded

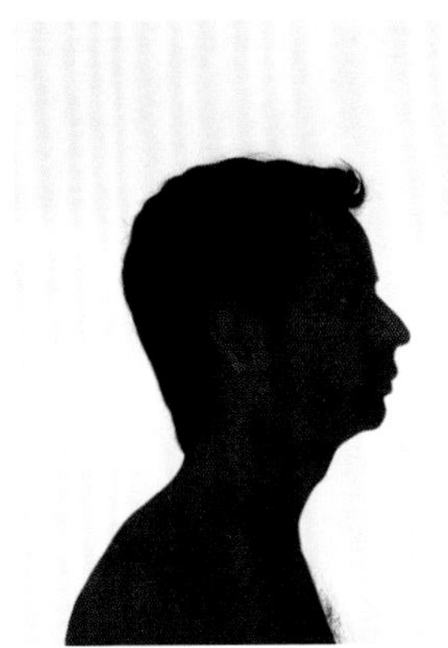

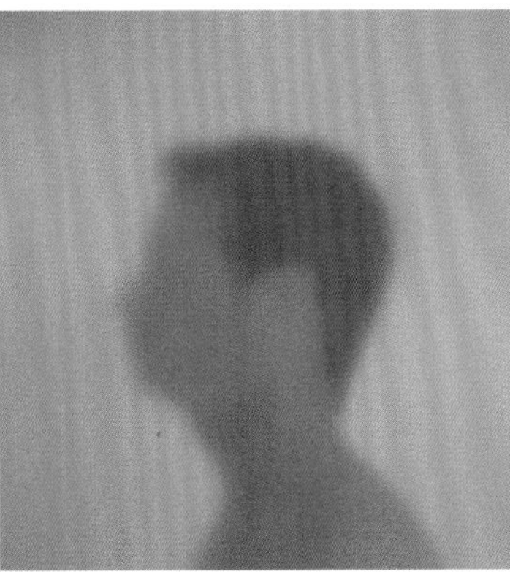

Ali Kazim, *Untitled (Self-portrait, diptych)*, 2012, watercolour pigment on paper and dry pigments on mylar, 45 x 78 cm
Collection of Taimur Hassan,©Ali Kazim, courtesy Jhaveri Contemporary

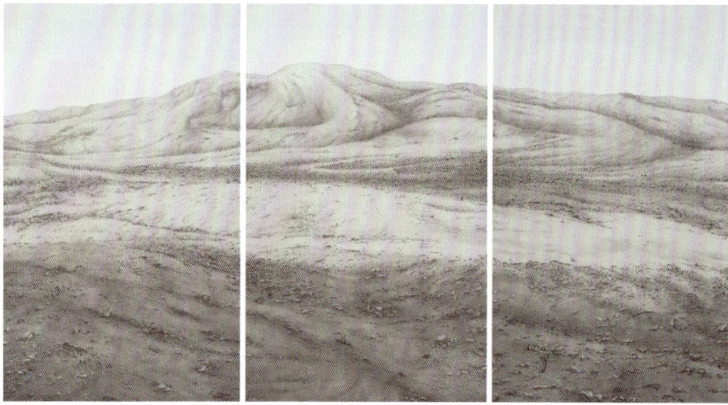

Ali Kazim, *Untitled (Ruins series, Triptych)*, 2018, watercolour pigment on paper, 193 x 358 cm

Collection of Sanda Lwin and Farhad Karim,©Ali Kazim, courtesy Jhaveri Contemporary

meanings associated with it, whether about fashion, gender or religion.

I constructed tube-like forms with human hair by using hair sprays. The structure resembled the internal structure of the body. I tried to install and suspend the work with fish wire – it looked terrible. In class discussion I learnt about how magicians use an invisible thread to trick their audiences, making it seem like a form is floating in space. I used this technique to create a 'moving drawing'. The slightest of movements around the object – for example someone passing by – resulted in it moving ever so lightly in space.

MKL: When did you first work on the wash technique?

AK: For my BA degree show, I used Winsor and Newton graphic inks available at the NCA. However, I realised that the inks fade with time. I try to resolve problems by working around the mechanics or conceptual issues. So I tried pigments. I studied the surface of Bengal School paintings in the Lahore Museum, and the atmospheric landscapes created with the wash technique.

MKL: Do you think living in Lahore and teaching at the NCA motivates and encourages your work today?

AK: If the hunger to learn, and be inspired and energised by the works of other artists is not fulfilled through some other avenue, it becomes important to feel grounded and know you are part of a community. Teaching at the NCA provides me with that sense of space and community. I teach as well as learn, but an institute can also provide a feeling of security.

MKL: The models or references for your

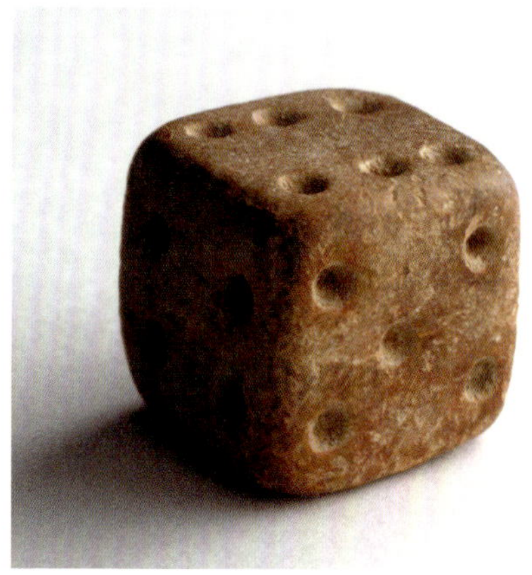

portraits are acquaintances, strangers and/or objects. Do you work with models in your studio? How do you choose your references?
AK: Models who fit a commercial beauty aesthetic make me nervous. I tend not to follow those standards, and re-imagine my chosen references. Ordinary people do not normally try to control others. I do feel people's personality, appearance and character can dominate me. I do not want the subject to influence me while I am working. If I want to change or experiment with details, I should be able to do this, without any external pressure. The subject is just a reference.
MKL: Due to your interest in the human skin, you painted portraits of semi-nude or nude figures. You are now painting figures with clothes. What has changed?
AK: I want the figures I portray to appear timeless. For example, my figures appeared wearing amulets, but not elements that would distinctly define their historic context. I refused to specify time through fashion, space and/or even light until 2009. I am now trying, on a lighter note, not to be too hard on myself. I want to break through my own boundaries.
MKL: Like most Mughal portraits, your subjects - usually a solitary single figure - do not normally make eye contact with the viewer. Are you declining the gaze of the observer?
AK: I feel the subject should engage the viewer rather than confront them. Profiles, features, details of the clothing etc. should invite the audience to look closely. When I have portrayed more than one figure, the interpretation has focused on their relationship or potential romance. A single figure is more about its inward-looking beauty and character.
MKL: The exhibition includes some of your earlier works, like *Ruins*. What interested you in these landscapes?
AK: Without a particular project in mind, I started to photograph Indus sherds in museum collections. I was fascinated by ancient fragments of utensils and in fossils - the process of fossilisation and preservation over time. I amassed a huge pile of photographs. Once back in Pakistan I started visiting unexcavated mounds, which have vast quantities of surface finds. The terracotta fragments

(right) Figure of a bull or ox, terracotta, 5.4 x 9.2 x 3.5 cm, Chanhu-daro, Pakistan, 2500–2300 BC
Ashmolean Museum, University of Oxford (EACh.1)

(opposite) Terracotta dice, terracotta, 2 cm square, Mohenjo-daro, Pakistan, 2500–1900 BC
Ashmolean Museum, University of Oxford (EAMd.25)

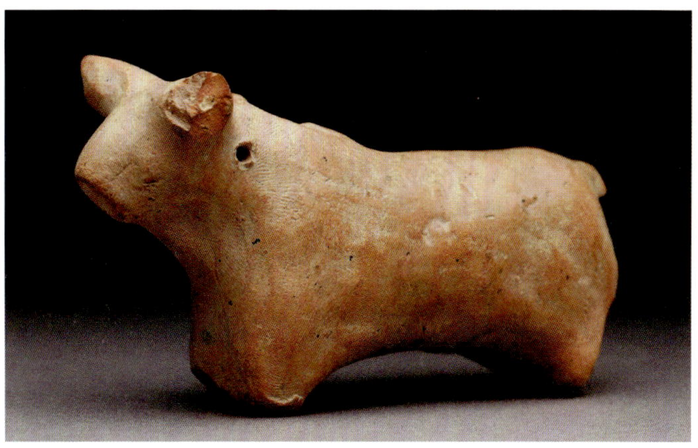

that covered the surface turned the landscape as red as Mars. I happened to pick up a sherd and saw a clear thumb print on it. It was an emotional moment to place my own thumb on the thumb print of an ancient artist - I felt like I was travelling back in time. However, the *Ruins* series is not the same landscape, but the result of piecing together photographs of sherds and landscapes - a composite of hundreds of images. An archaeologist would look at the landscape scientifically, while I looked at it and developed my own space.

MKL: Your monochrome landscapes focus on spaces without people, whereas the portraits in high contrasting colours have figures in a conceptual void. Why are your landscapes monochrome?

AK: Just like *Conference of Birds*, which I first attempted in colour, I have also attempted landscapes in colour. Birds in colour became more about the birds. Their details dominated the piece, rather than the idea behind the work. *Ruins* in colour didn't work for me either. Until 2009 I used colours in my work, but after 2009 I made just a couple of portraits in colour. For almost a decade, there was an absence of colour in my work. It was also a period where I focused on materials such as hair and clay.

MKL: I tend to connect your *Self-Portrait with Cloud*, *Ruins* and *Conference of Birds*. Visually they are all in monochrome but for me there is also introspection. What were your thoughts when painting the landscapes?

AK: When I painted the landscapes, I also played and worked with clay. I thought about Indus terracotta artefacts as records of the past. The emphasis was on firing ceramics and slipware, while also painting the landscapes. However, I do believe the *Ruins* series, with its fragments, is a collective portrait of and about ancient people. The *Ruins* are not regular landscapes - I see the series as a memorial to those who lived at these ancient sites.

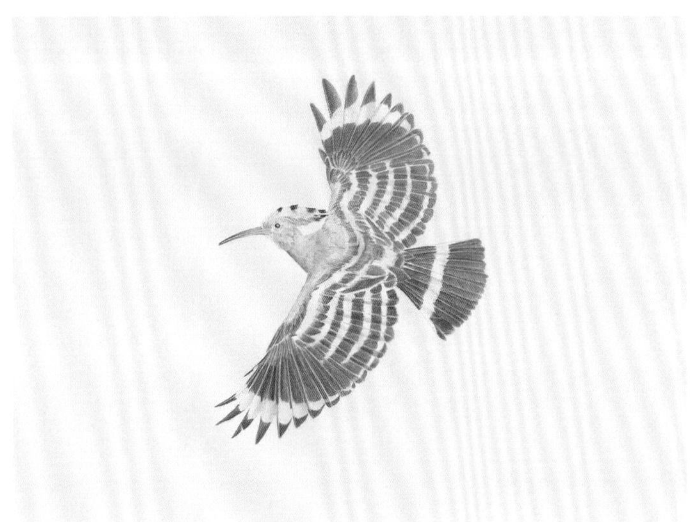

Ali Kazim, *Conference of Birds, in 5 parts* (detail), 2019, watercolour pigments on paper, 198 x 570 cm
©Ali Kazim, courtesy Jhaveri Contemporary

MKL: Is *Conference of Birds* - as a relationship between humans, birds, animals and the environment - a new phase or trajectory in your work?
AK: Possibly, as it is a way of following my heart. The poem *Conference of Birds* is beautiful, but equally compelling are the stories and myths associated with the Sufi poet 'Attar's life. To almost destroy oneself in search of something true - whether these were the Birds, 'Attar or the Buddha - is overwhelming to consider.
MKL: How do you describe your installation in Lahore of unfired clay birds that dissolved in the rain last year?
AK: At the start of their journey, 'Attar says the birds filled the sky. Slowly some fall back, tempted by new aspects of life; others are captured by beasts. Just 30 survive in the end. However, the entire flock was responsible for the courage necessary to start the journey. All the birds are important, not just the final 30 heroes. The installation of 3,000 unfired clay birds commemorated all the unsung, unnamed heroes of a large collective. Not everyone makes it in life, but everyone deserves to be remembered. Those who have encouraged us, supported us and nourished us should not be forgotten.
MKL: Is there a link between the Lahore installation and the sinister *Bird Hunter*?
AK: One of my references was the Indus Delta, where migratory birds come to rest and people hunt them. In *Conference of Birds*, we look at human life through birds. In the *Hunter* series, we see humans trap birds. The birds no longer speak for mankind, and humans control their survival or extinction.
MKL: Why did you arrange self-portraits as the demonic Mara's army?
AK: Several things have been helpful in shedding my doubts and inhibitions, including conversations with you. The self-portraits were an attempt to return to painting multiple figures. Mara's army helped to break my self-imposed constraints. I also thought about the

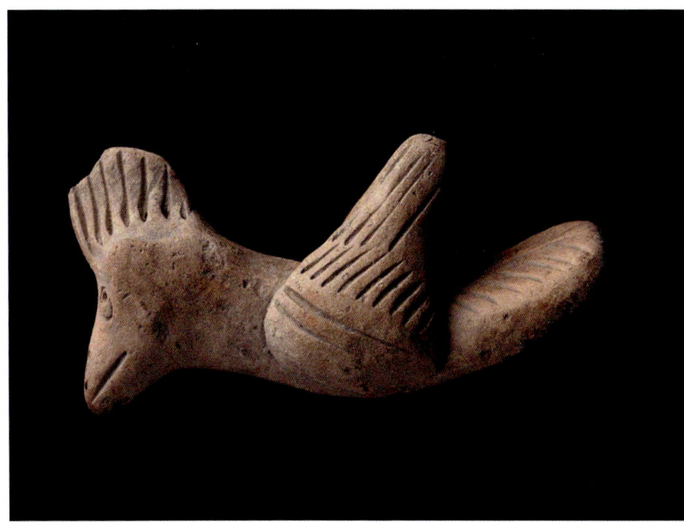

Terracotta figure of a bird, terracotta, 5.2 cm, Khotan, China, 301–600 AD
Ashmolean Museum, University of Oxford (EAX.1)

demons within us, those that scare us, the ones we fear most. Bulleh Shah says: *"You have not fought your own demons, your own desires, the ones who live in your heart."*
MKL: What about the mourner figure?
AK: I looked closely at the *Gandharan Mourner* in the Ashmolean. I saw a young man in pain, almost as if he was self-punishing. I asked someone in Lahore to pose, focusing specifically on the posture and hands. The *Gandharan Mourner* has such visible grief etched on his face, body and posture. Perhaps young Siddhartha encountered a similar grief-stricken mourner when he first saw a dead body.
MKL: Why do you think it is important for you to work across different formats and materials?
AK: It is really important that the material relates to the idea. I first envisioned *Conference of Birds* installation in ash, or fired pieces. But ultimately unfired clay seemed the appropriate material for the birds. I favour material that absorbs the audience.
MKL: Which artists have most influenced your work?
AK: I have focused on that what is available in Pakistan - Gandharan and Mughal art. Alas, those artists remain mostly anonymous, other than Nainsukh, whose work I admire greatly. There are the haunting works of Mehmed Siyah-Kalem (15th century, Iran). I admire Doris Salcedo, Kiki Smith, Louise Bourgeois, Cornelia Parker, Mona Hatoum, Vija Celmins and Robert Gober. Besides Gober, most artists I admire happen to be women. There is a certain intimacy in their works - a touch, a soul that I don't see in the works of most popular male artists.
MKL: In your view, what are some of the Western misconceptions about art in Pakistan, or more generally the subcontinent?
AK: Currently the West does not think of art and culture when it thinks about Pakistan. People often associate the country with bearded men and the Taliban. The media is responsible for this representation; in movies, Pakistanis are often villains. I think that until the discipline of the study of art history includes equal reference to the East, Pakistan will remain on the artistic periphery. Also, European and North American museums focus mainly on Western art, and museum galleries dedicated to the East are often at the back or side of the building. More recently, some South Asian artists have been offered gallery space and exhibitions, but overall I do not think there is proportional representation in museums, despite large diaspora. If we artists on the subcontinent focus more on the development and distribution of our work at a global level, it will help change such issues with representation.

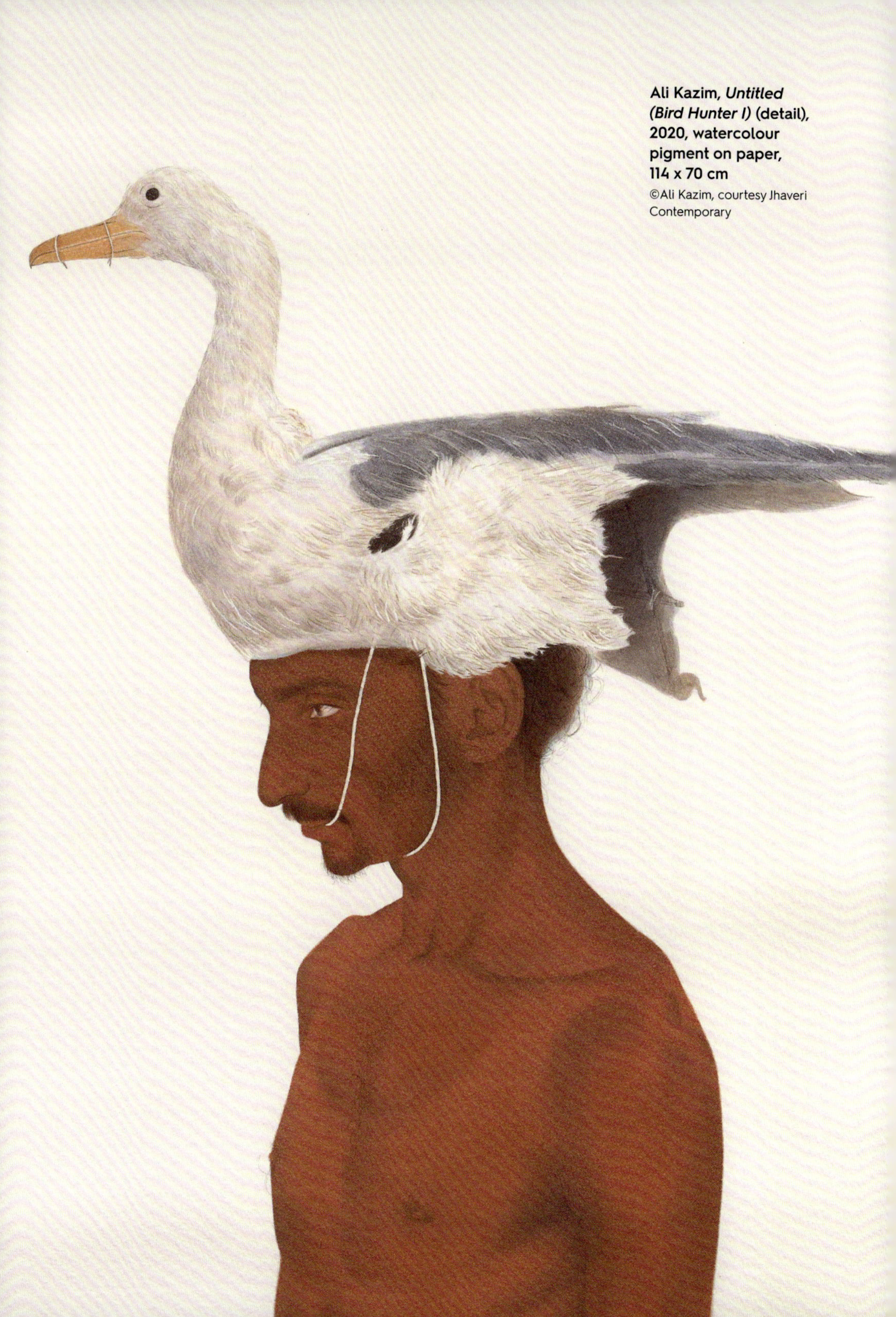

Ali Kazim, *Untitled (Bird Hunter I)* (detail), 2020, watercolour pigment on paper, 114 x 70 cm

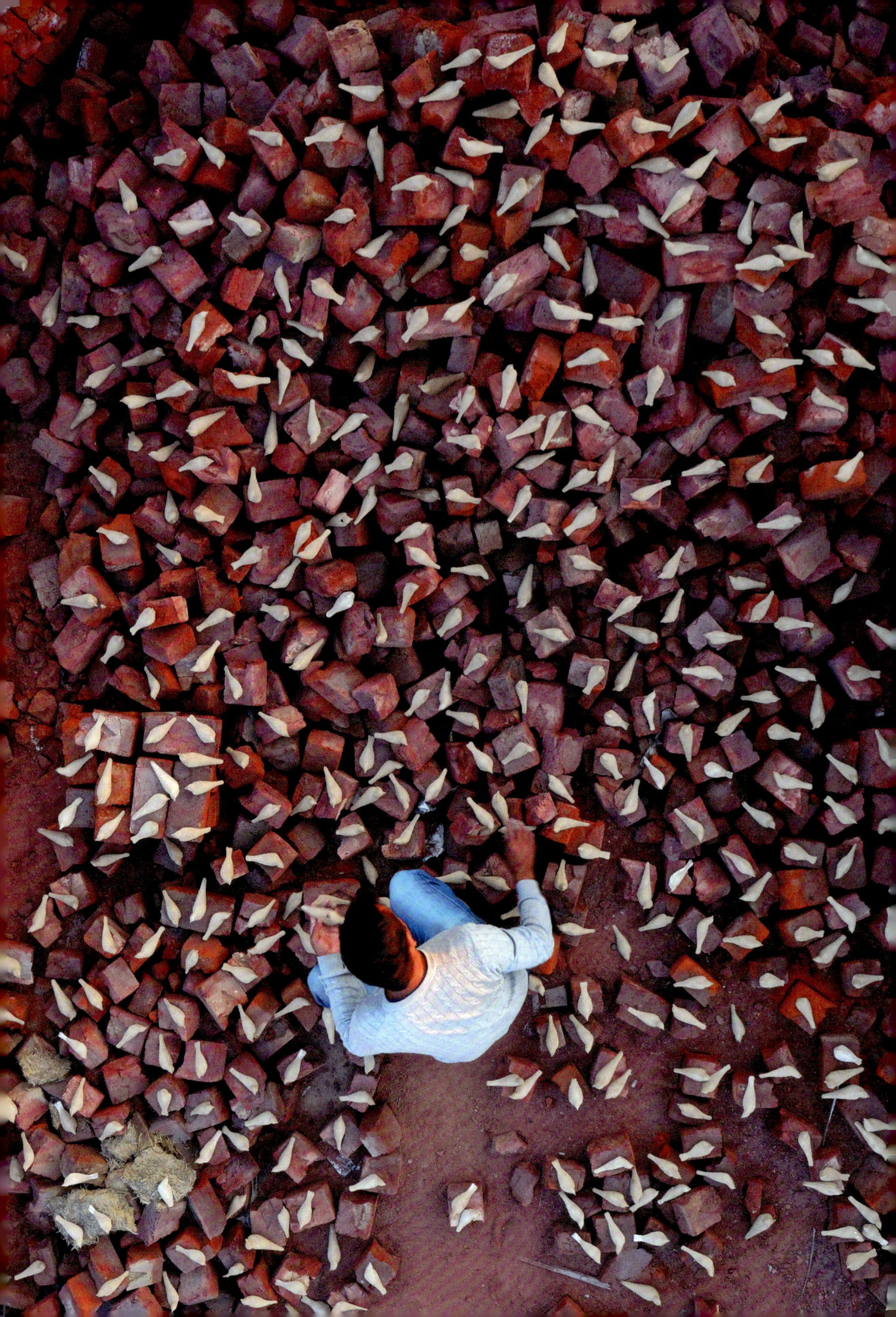

Tim Hitchens

SOUTH ASIA: OPENING OUR EYES TO OURSELVES

THERE ARE SOME EXHIBITIONS which blow away the dusty cobwebs of preconception, and this is one.

Having lived in Pakistan for three years, and with family who live there now, I am all too aware of the gap between the European image of contemporary Pakistan and the reality. The country, and its people, can too easily be pigeon-holed into the contested phenomena of religious radicalism, terrorism and sustainable development. But as the work of Ali Kazim illustrates, Pakistan is much more contemporary, and much more ancient, than we tend to think.

Ali comes from a modest town - Pattoki, in central Punjab - and he is by all accounts a modest man. His artistry began in the commercial world of painting circus hoardings. But his home is also close to Harappa, one of the great cities of the 5,000-year-old Indus Valley civilisation, and the inspiration for his work comes as much from there as it does contemporary Pakistan. His visit to the Harappan sites in 2013 was clearly a transformational moment, and *The Ruins* series which followed reaches back to the deep, pre-Islamic traditions of the territory which is now Pakistan. An abiding love of terracotta followed, and a sense of both the lasting power and fragility of clay. One can see this again in the 2020 installation of 3,000 unbaked clay birds at an abandoned brick factory in Lahore, which lasted until the rain fell and the clay birds turned once more to earth.

Lahore Biennale 2020, *Conference of Birds*, installation
©Ali Kazim

Ali's work also draws on the traditions of Company School drawings – the mutual artistic learning which came from the early days of the East India Company in India (captured for British audiences in 2019 at the *Forgotten Masters: Indian Painting for the East India Company* exhibition at the Wallace Collection.) That period, perhaps too easily romanticised, nevertheless showed a willingness on the part of British officials in the late eighteenth and early nineteenth centuries to learn from the artistry and accomplishment of Indian master painters. Ali's own portraits draw on that line of expertise: 'The subject is just in focus, and everything else is left', as he puts it himself. There is a pregnant depth to the pictures, which often leave pure colour to do much of the emotional work of the pieces – a powerful emptiness not dissimilar to those of his Harappan landscapes, void of humans but full of human history. I particularly appreciate his *Man of Faith* and *Woman of Faith* series, portraits of people of religious faith which are highly contemporary and sympathetic; how often in Europe do you now see religious pictures which are so simple, direct and warm?

These works, as I say, should change our perception of contemporary Pakistan and Pakistanis. But they should also change our perceptions of Britain and Britishness.

After the Lahore National College of Arts, Ali studied at the Slade in London. Though he enjoyed his time there, I like his comment that 'the city had more to offer than the school' – this is a good generalisation, which could also apply to a university city like Oxford. At their best, London and Oxford are not British cities at all, but global and international hubs. It is important that artists like Ali feel at home in both cities. And it is important that everyone in Britain, especially post-Brexit, understands what it is to be British in the twenty-first century. Recognising how multi-ethnic, for example how South Asian we have become is a key to that understanding. South Asia is not other, but now a significant part of ourselves. The largest ethnic minority in Oxford is British Pakistani. In this city we are as close to Birmingham as we are to London. In 2016, 7.2% of UK domiciled students at this university identified as Asian; by 2020 that figure had risen to

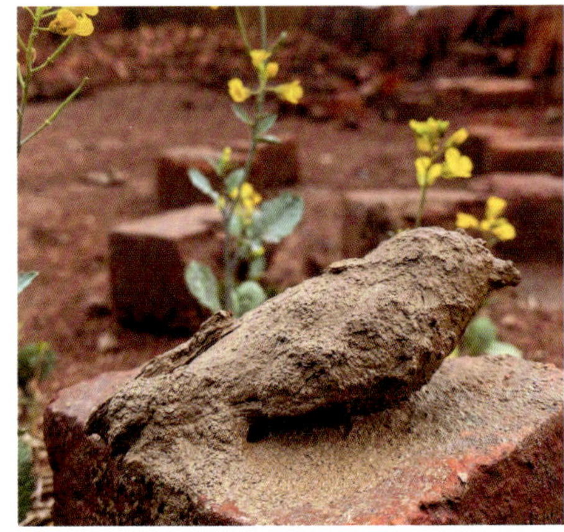

Lahore Biennale, 2020, *Conference of Birds*, installation (after the rain)
©Ali Kazim

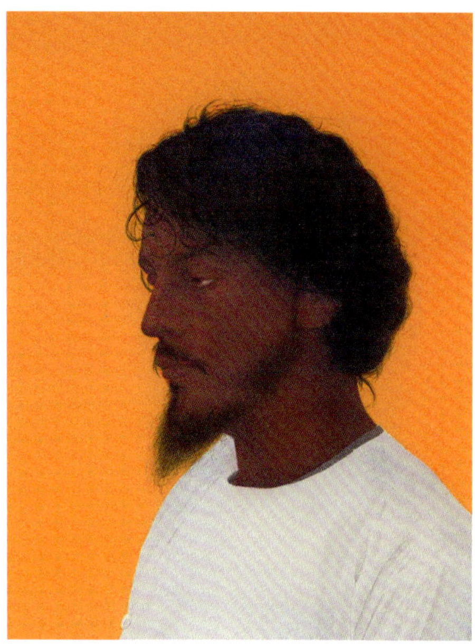

Ali Kazim, *Untitled (Man of Faith Series)* (detail), 2019, watercolour pigment on paper, 114 x 80 cm

©Ali Kazim, courtesy Jhaveri Contemporary

9.6%. One in ten of our British students is now Asian, to say nothing of our international student body.

When I became President of Wolfson College four years ago, in 2018, it was clear to me that our Oxford collegiate University would thrive if it recognised how international we were. Oxford should not be a comfortable place to observe the world from, but a rigorous place to observe the world in. If wisdom and knowledge - the aims of a university - come from perspective, then perspective comes from seeing many different perspectives. Our colleges need to - and at their best do - provide a recognisable home for our multinational and multicultural student and researcher body. More than half the students at Oxford are now graduate students, and at least two-thirds of our graduate students are from overseas. At Wolfson we have tried, in part through our art collection, to create an environment which is as welcoming to our Ugandan, Bangladeshi or Peruvian students as it is to our American, German or British ones. The Ashmolean has generously lent us a nineteenth-century marble statue from west India of Ganesha, the 'Lord of New Beginnings' and God of wisdom and learning, who greets all our students on their arrival.

And in parallel, it is thoroughly welcome that the Ashmolean is putting on this exhibition which shows the work of a young, brilliant, contemporary South Asian artist. British museums and galleries can sometimes fall into a pattern of showing contemporary works from Europe and North America, and more retrospective or historical views of work from Asia. It's the sign of a vigorous museum that it is able and willing to share with us what is happening now - in Asia's art world, and in Asian culture.

This exhibition can open our eyes to South Asia, and open our eyes to ourselves. Ali Kazim is a wonderful guide.

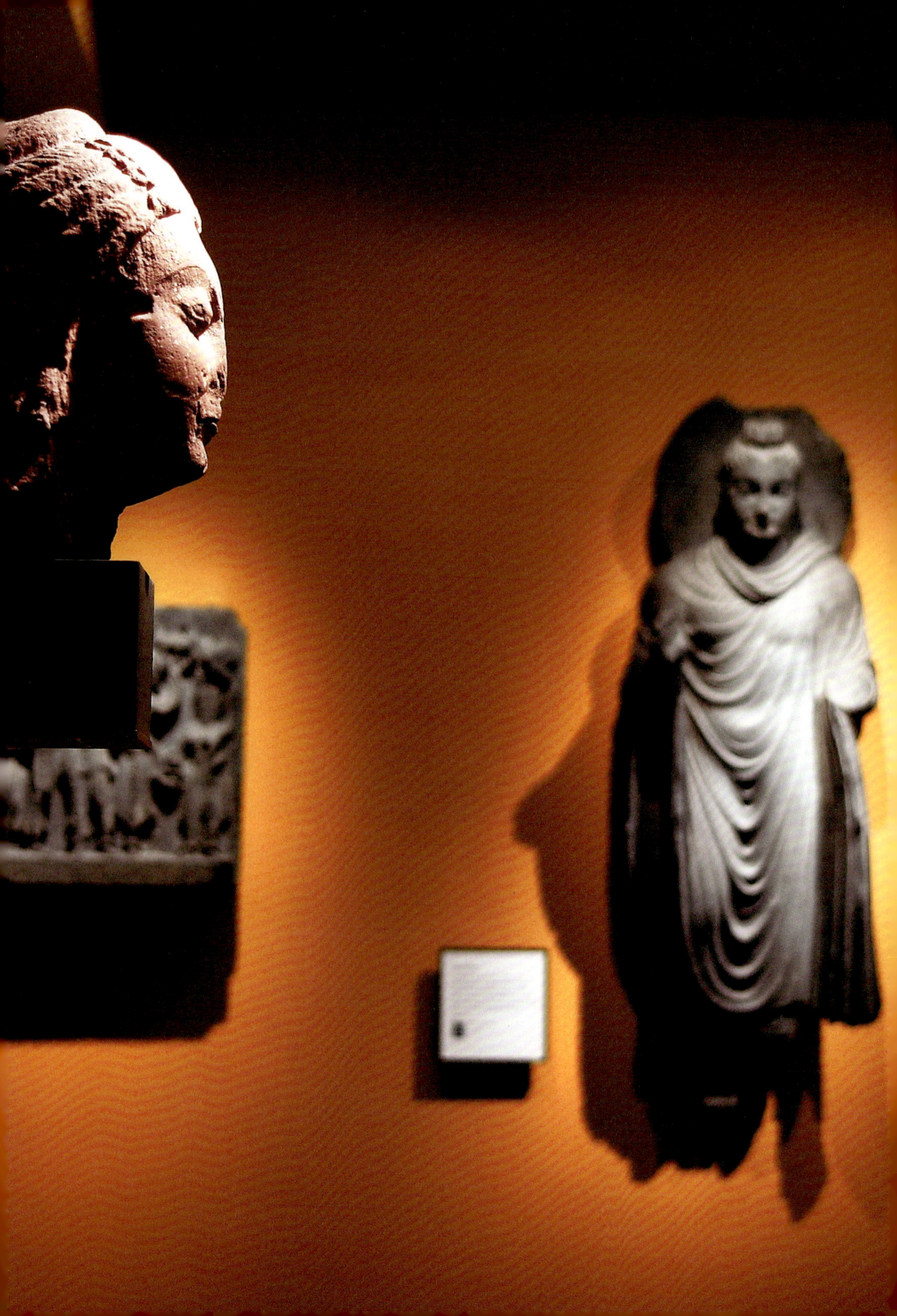

Faisal Devji

THE MUSEUM IS OPEN

WHILE AT THE ASHMOLEAN, Ali Kazim made use of the Museum's artefacts in his practice. Many of these, including Gandharan statuary as well as Mughal and British colonial objects from South Asia, had come to the Ashmolean from the old Indian Institute. Established in Oxford with Indian donations in the 1880s, the Institute's collections had been used to showcase the empire and train colonial officials. Kazim brought the vibrant aesthetic culture of modern Pakistan into the Ashmolean by engaging with these objects. His art serves as a meditation on their history, while turning them to new ends in a relationship about continuity as much as change. Could there be a better way of reflecting upon the fiery debates about race and colonialism that mark today's culture wars?

The University of Oxford has been at the centre of these debates. The 'Rhodes Must Fall' movement began in South Africa in 2015, in protest against the legacy of colonialism and racism. Confined to universities, its supporters attacked the symbols of this past, focusing on statues of Cecil Rhodes, the empire-builder and notable donor to educational causes. But the movement also stimulated conversations about changing the ways academic institutions work. By 2016 the movement had arrived in Oxford, and was calling for the removal of the statue of Rhodes at Oriel College, where he had studied and to which he subsequently donated a large sum of money. The college's governing body

Ashmolean Gallery view

did, following an inquiry, vote to remove the statue and change its procedures to promote racial equality and diversity.

In 2020 the killing of an African American man called George Floyd by police in Minneapolis propelled the 'Black Lives Matter' movement far beyond US borders and the limited Commonwealth history and university contexts of 'Rhodes Must Fall'. But it also took from the latter the practice of pulling down statues, which focused in the US on some Confederate commemorations of the Civil War, as well as on institutional monuments and titles associated with racism. Across the UK, 'Black Lives Matter' supporters attacked statues of slavers and political figures deemed to be racist, which re-ignited protests against Rhodes in Oxford.

The government responded by making alteration to monuments more difficult as part of an effort to preserve the nation's history, and so Oriel suspended the removal of its Rhodes statue, citing 'regulatory and financial challenges'. Whatever one's opinion of these developments, the controversy has focused people's thinking about the past, and how to deal with its symbols as well as its consequences. Was the effort to topple Rhodes simply meant to draw attention to continuing racial inequalities in modern Britain, or did it also constitute a statement about what kind of public history this country should have? Ought colonial monuments to be contextualised, placed in museums, or removed altogether?

In other words, museums and public memory have become crucial to such debates, whose controversies sometimes help – and at other times hinder – the quiet work of reforming procedures, revising curricula, and diversifying hiring and admissions at British universities. The national tradition of putting up a principled front against demands of forceful change – while accepting and modulating such change in retrospect or behind the scenes – was stymied by the renewal of protests over Rhodes between 2016 and 2021. These protests, moreover, seemed to refer to museums merely as sites for the display and understanding of a dead past, where colonial statuary should be mothballed.

The distinction between a dead past in museums and a living present on the streets is one that museology has fought for decades; it was strange to have this old-fashioned and arguably colonial view voiced by the 'Rhodes Must Fall' movement. Meanwhile, the government, in advocating for the status quo, appeared in favour of treating public space as a museum. Both sides in the debate, then, paradoxically agreed on what

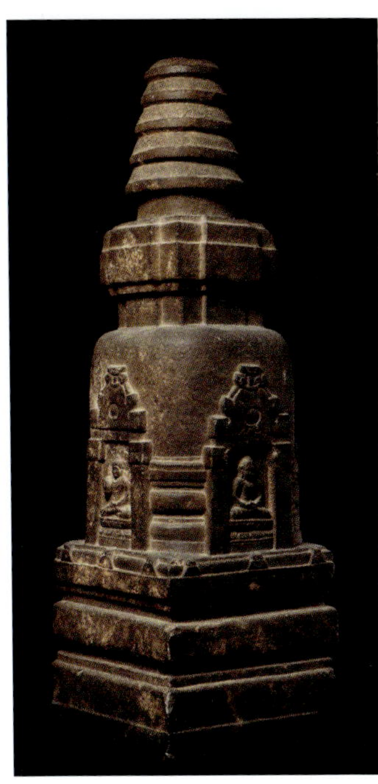

Votive stupa, stone, 78 x 44 x 35 cm, Bodh Gaya, India, 701–800 AD
Ashmolean Museum, University of Oxford (EAOS.57)

museums were for. In Oxford there was even a proposal to establish a museum of colonialism in a city that could be seen by tourists as an open-air museum of imperial history.

Away from this stereotyped debate about the past, however, museums have begun to address the issues raised by such controversies in more productive ways. Ali Kazim, for instance, was the first South Asian artist in residence at the University of Oxford, and the first living artist from the region to have a solo show at the Ashmolean. His work there did not seek to address the history of colonial collections just by contextualising artefacts and marking their links with empire (as if in retribution). Instead, it made the Museum's collections into a site and source of new artistic production. Kazim does not relabel the past, but uses the Ashmolean to inspire the creation of a truly post-colonial culture in the present.

While clearly South Asian in its subject matter, Kazim's work is not marked by any tropes of nationalist or civilisational authenticity. Rather than opposing some colonial or Western representations of Asian society by invoking a more authentic reality, he evades such cultural distinctions and identities to show us the sometimes fraught - but also mixed and common - worlds in which we live. His presence at the Ashmolean has allowed the Museum's South Asian collections to live again in the present - not as the artefacts of a national or civilisational identity, but as the building blocks of a new future.

By connecting the past at the Ashmolean to the present - and linking this to a future in the countries of South and Central Asia - Ali Kazim's exhibition offers the Museum's audience a new sense of living history. But it also invites the participation of distinct new audiences such as Oxford's large Pakistani community, which might not otherwise see itself reflected in the Ashmolean's collections at all. Kazim's presence and work at the Museum makes contemporary India and Pakistan - the first countries to gain independence from Britain in the twentieth century - visible in a new way, and to a new audience. Here, then, is a response to one of the great cultural debates of our times.

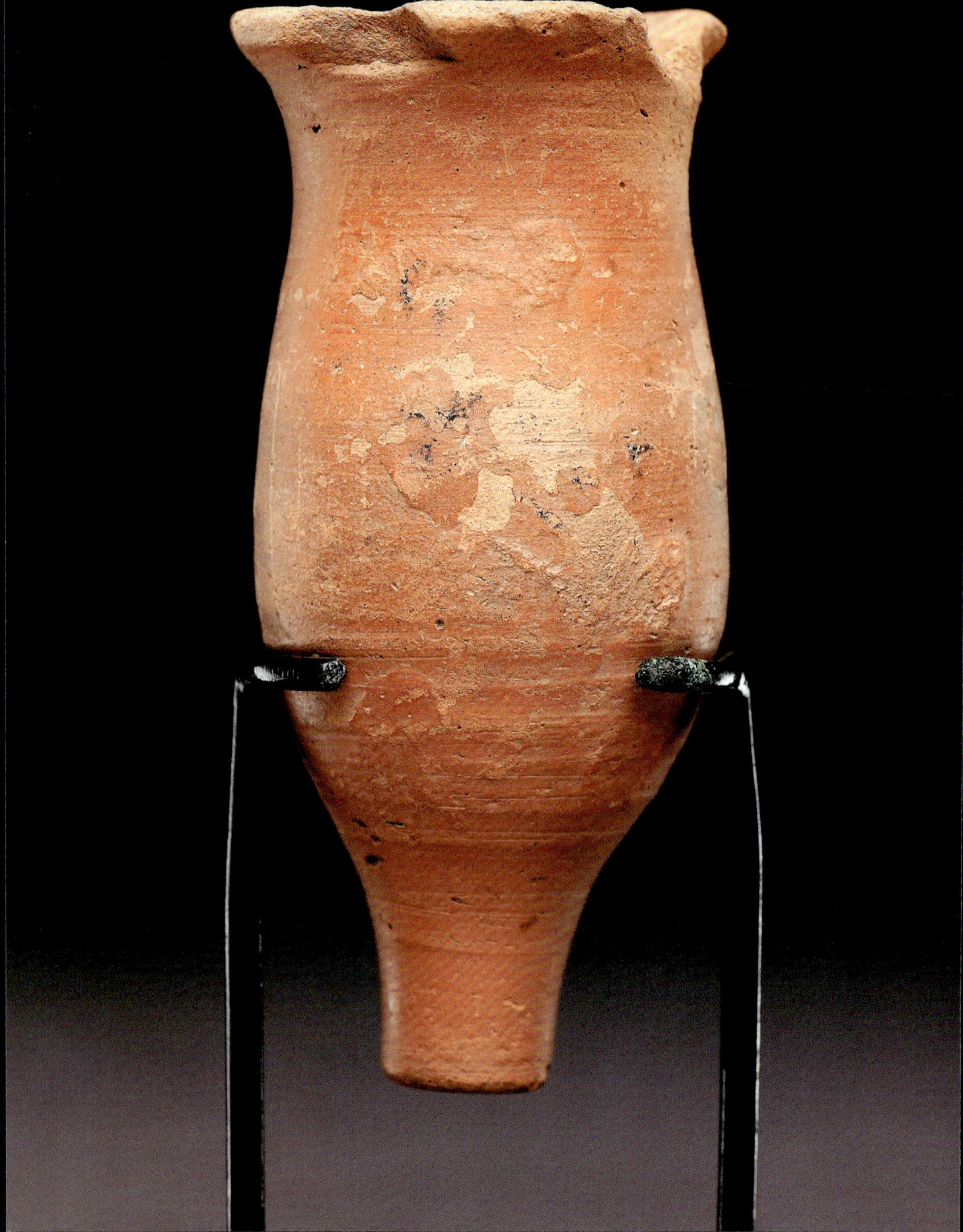

Emilia Terracciano

ALI KAZIM'S SERIES *RUINS*

The sun and the moon are asleep in every speck of your dust
Though innumerable other gems are also hidden in your dust
- Iqbal

PAINTER AND POTTER ALI KAZIM has long been drawn to ancient sites for their symbolic value and archaeological resonance. Over the years, starting some time in 2006, he began making photographic records of ancient objects encountered in public collections located the world over: the Lahore Museum, the Victoria and Albert Museum and the Metropolitan. He photographed numerous artefacts, ranging from utilitarian objects such as clay pots, to less prosaic items, for example, jewellery to sacred terracotta votive figurines. Some useful, others beautiful, these objects had been designed and handled by ancient peoples: Harappans, Mesopotamians and Egyptians, civilisations that had settled, flourished and eventually perished alongside riverine regions of historic strategic importance. For centuries, the Indus, Euphrates, Tigris and Nile nurtured and sustained life, before plants disappeared due to draught, sand dunes crept close to settlements, and drier climates depleted basins.

Kazim completed an MA in London in 2012, and upon his return to Pakistan the idea of creating a record of ruins gradually accreted. Regular visits to unexcavated sites in and around his hometown, Lahore, ignited his imagination. Located on the banks

Small terracotta flask, terracotta, 8.7 cm Indus Valley, 2500–1900 BC
Ashmolean Museum, University of Oxford (EAX.7289)

of the Indus, these lands were inhabited between 2700–1900 BC by the Harappan, the earliest known urban culture of the Indian subcontinent. Reconstructions based on ethno-archaeology and studies of techiniques of terracotta indicate that Harappans fired the soft, blackish clay of the river bank, more pliable owing to its underwater location.

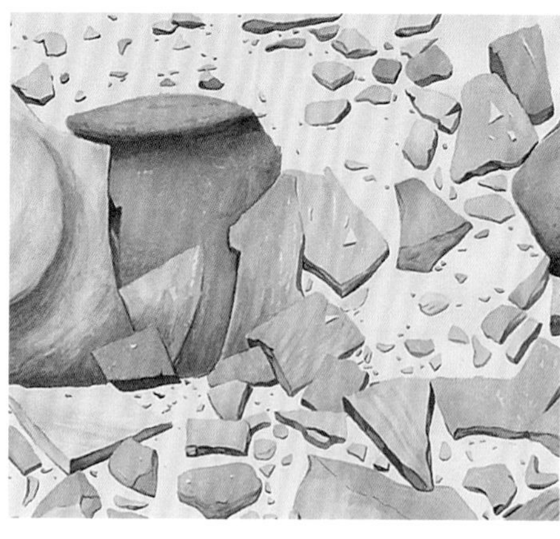

Ali Kazim, *Untitled (Ruins IIII)* (detail), 2016, watercolour pigment on paper, 75 x 114 cm
©Ali Kazim, courtesy Jhaveri Contemporary

Kazim recounts how some of the sites he visited around Lahore took on otherworldly connotations. Moreover, he noticed how the surrounding landscape had been altered by the presence of terracotta fragments left by humans long ago; sherds varying in size and shape were scattered everywhere, tingeing the soil a deep, warm red. He started to experiment, wishing to visualise traces of these landscapes in a more literal sense. The series *Ruins* - composed of untitled studies of the Harappan landscapes - resulted in a carefully painted body of work (*Ruins* II and *Ruins* III). Producing both a tonal grey landscape and one composed of single and identifiable sherds, Kazim reconstructed each scene with forensic attentiveness. Using tracing paper, and then polyester film, or Mylar, he began by placing it on top of individual pottery fragments to create physical records - tracings - of the various shapes. It took him considerable time, Kazim explains, to understand the process of Mylar, how the material responded to pigments. The result was a visual rendition in which each sherd retains a semblance of its past use. Upon inspection, the viewer is cast in the role of an inquisitive archaeologist who can speculate about the clues on view, advance conclusions about the shape the complete object once held and be prompted to image the relationship between part and the whole. What was the function of this fragment? Was the object designed for cooking or simply for storage? Was it stacked along with several others? Did it come with handles, or a lid? How did the human body manipulate it?

Contemplating *Ruins* offers an eerie experience. Perhaps inevitably, sherds evoke bone fragments and open-air burial sites. In this series Kazim produced four further chiaroscuro landscapes on large panels (134 x 342 cm) which seemingly invite the viewer to take an imaginary walk amongst the ruins on display. Composed of three large panels, *Untitled (Ruins series)* is inspired by abstract photographic references. The grisaille landscape does not depict a specific site and in some way, it could be said that it is fictional. Kazim used natural pigments and water, explaining that he wished to give an impression of the passing of time, and of the traces left by expired civilisations through the process itself. The repeated and careful application of layers of natural pigments - dust diluted in water - hints both at the inherent composition of Kazim's chosen materials (ground, oxidised minerals and metals) and at the dual properties of this pulverised medium, its potential to create and preserve traces, but also ultimately to destroy them. He writes: 'Everything that is made by humans in these [Harappan] landscapes comes from the earth, from dust. The remains of old bricks, the fragments of pottery, they are all made from the earth itself, from clay, and from what will eventually become dust.' Yet Kazim also reminds the viewer that if you add water to dust or soil, it is as if you are converting dust to clay: what is unformed can become formed, and vice versa. Through the process of combustion, moreover, the firing of clay fixes the form and shape of the object and its usage, that is, how the human will adapt it. Kazim the potter alludes to the fact that the domestication of fire brought about the re-organisation of the natural world for human control and convenience; it cleared the land, but also made plants and animals more palatable, bringing them into a tighter circle around the *domus*, the hearth. Archaeologists regard the terracotta pot and the granary as the first indisputable signs of sedentariness - of the home.

Ruins offers contrasting impressions of time and its passing: of the vanity of life, its ineluctable finitude, but also of the strange and magnetic appeal of dust and its potential to stimulate research and speculation. Objects of archaeological study typically call to mind the past, yet these grisaille images are also about the future. Lingering and wandering over these landscapes, we become more aware of our relationship to the environment on this planet. *Ruins* prompts one to interrogate the value of life amidst the ruins that are yet to materialise, those of the future - environmental collapse linked to exhaustive resource extraction and anthropogenic climate change. If the ruins of the future seem closer in time and space than those of the Harappans, then we are led to contemplate what might be our collective residue in the landscape yet to come. Should we be succeeded by another civilisation, we may, on passing through the alchemist's hands, become part of someone's painting, landscape, or even a pot! But this fate is not yet secured for us.

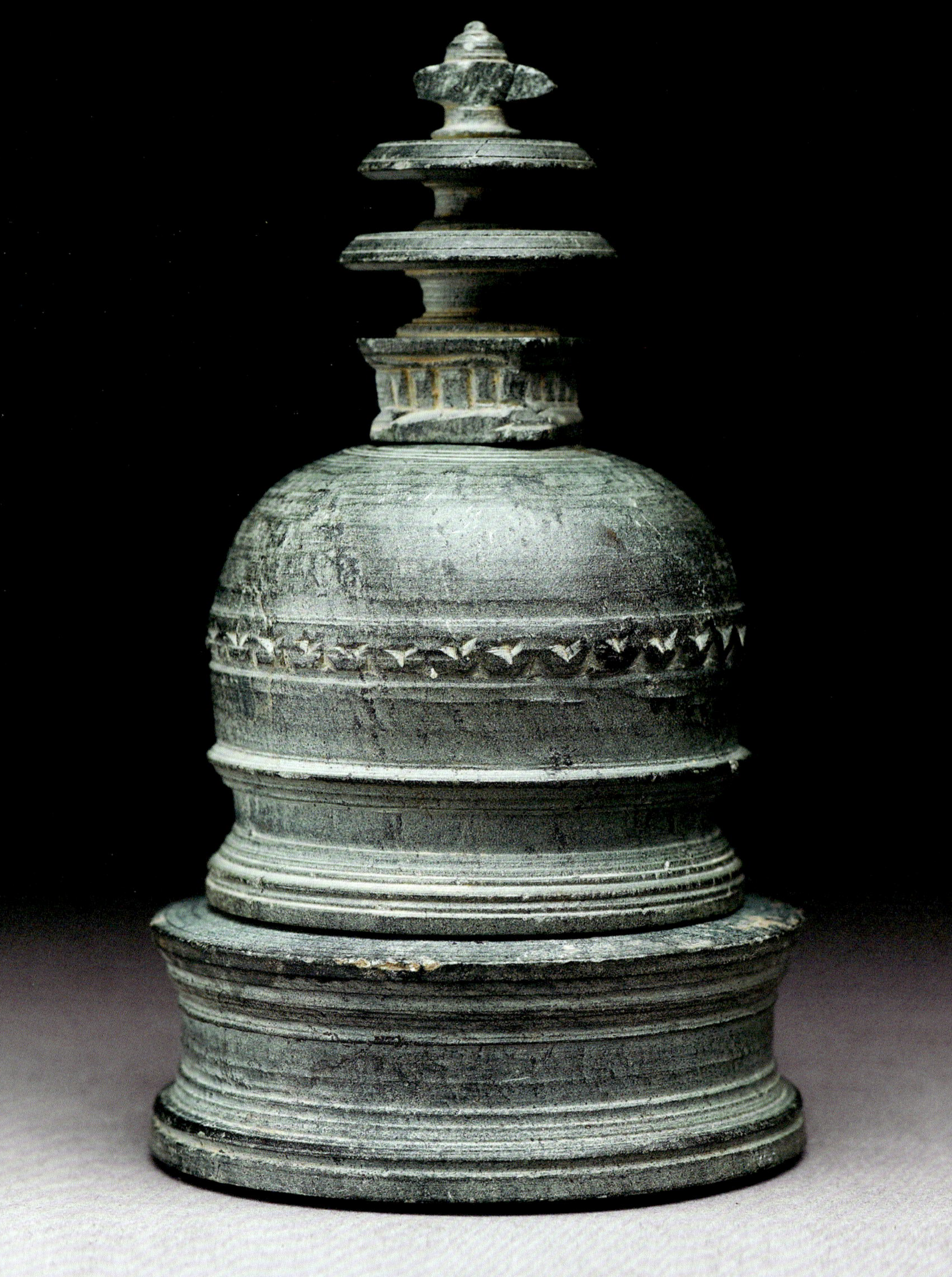

Peter Stewart

ALI KAZIM AND ARCHAEOLOGY

FROM NEOLITHIC MEHRGARH AND the Bronze Age civilization of the Indus Valley, to the sculpted monuments of ancient Buddhism, the archaeology of pre-Islamic Pakistan has been one of the most consistent themes in Ali Kazim's work. Antiquities have offered him a richly varied visual vocabulary for conjuring up new, imaginary worlds. Landscapes encrusted with pottery sherds are pregnant with implications about the people who produced them. Ceramic sculptures in the shape of human hearts are used to form foundation walls. Meticulous drawings animate fragments of ancient reliefs.

Archaeologists are also in the business of extrapolating from fragmentary clues. The traces left behind by ancient societies resist interpretation (which is part of the discipline's appeal). They are the tantalising tip of the iceberg of what has been lost in the course of centuries, or indeed as a consequence of haphazard excavation or illicit digging in modern times. The evidence of fragments is often confusing or frustrating, and ancient images speak a language which we only half comprehend. Kazim understands well the attraction and the challenge of archaeological remains. In his work, there is a palpable sense that the significance of artefacts lies just out of reach, but at the same time, antiquities and ruins have an inherent beauty and fascination that prompts the artist to reinvent them.

Reliquary in the form of a stupa, grey schist, 2.5 cm, Gandhara, c.1–100 AD
Ashmolean Museum, University of Oxford (EA1978.127)

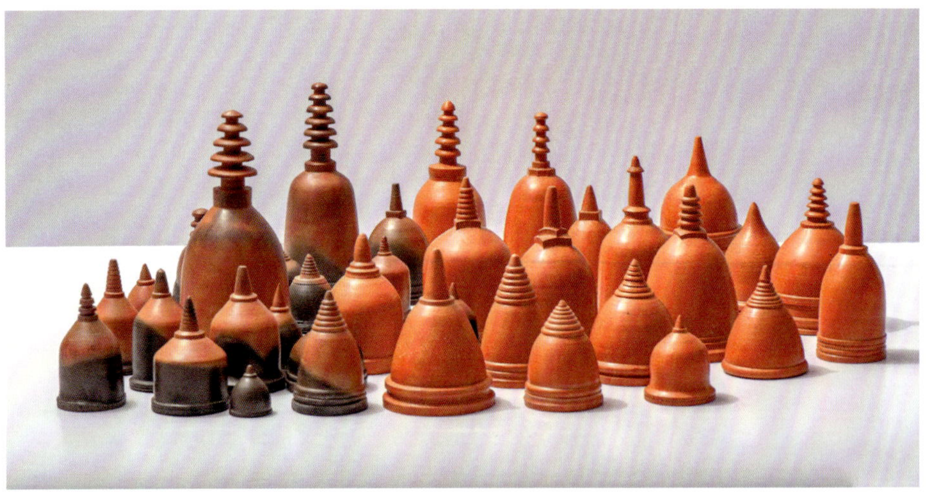

Ali Kazim, ***Untitled (Votive Objects)*, 2020, clay, various dimensions**

Gandharan art has been a particular focus of Kazim's work, notably during his 2019 Ashmolean/CARC (Classical Art Research Centre) residency in Oxford. This gave him the opportunity to spend time with South Asian antiquities from the Museum's reserve collections, as well as those on public display. His home city also contains one of the most important Gandharan collections of all, that of the venerable Lahore Museum. Gandhara is the ancient name for a region roughly centred on the northernmost tip of what is now Pakistan, around the Peshawar Valley and the surrounding mountains. This was one of the heartlands of ancient Buddhism in the early centuries AD. For much of this period Gandhara was part of the Kushan Empire, which controlled vast territories across Central Asia and northern India. The Kushans had contacts and common interests with the Roman Empire to the west; the people of Gandhara may have prospered as a result of the trade routes that crossed the region, linking the Indian subcontinent and the Arabian Sea with the 'Silk Road' of Central Asia. It was in this context that Gandharan Buddhists converted their worldly wealth into monumental monasteries and shrines, sumptuously adorned with painted figural sculptures in stone or plaster.

As in other parts of the ancient Buddhist world, Gandharan artworks provided a focus for veneration as well as a channel for pious donations. They represented a mixture of iconic devotional subjects - the Buddha himself and other revered figures - and more complicated, intricate scenes, particularly stories from the Buddha's historical life and past lives. Their principal purpose was the decoration of the *stupa*, which was central to the visitor's experience of sacred sites. The *stupa* was a reliquary shrine, often small but sometimes colossal in scale. It was a place to hold physical relics directly or indirectly associated with the Buddha. It took the form of a mound or 'dome', adorned at the top with sculpted umbrellas (*chatras*) - an architectural form that would later evolve into the pagodas of East Asia. One extraordinary stone reliquary casket in the Ashmolean's collection takes the shape of the sort of *stupa* in which it would itself presumably have been interred.

This repertoire of devotional art and architecture provides some of the ingredients for Ali Kazim's recent work. The resonant imagery of the Gandharan narrative reliefs and ancient *stupas* are appropriated and semi-detached from their origins, though still archaeologically recognisable. Sometimes this is a process of abstraction. The essential form of the *stupa* replicated in donors' reliquary caskets has been stripped of all the superficial decorative elements which ancient Buddhists would have expected in the real monument. Instead, Kazim's *Untitled (Votive Objects)* has transformed the ancient caskets into suggestive, minimalist forms. These beautiful and tactile miniature sculptures mimic the ancient shapes in orange clay. Each has a residual *chatra*. The archaeological allusion is there for the taking, but these offerings do not demand interpretation. We can speculate freely about which devotees left them, and for whom.

In other works, the ancient imagery has taken on a life of its own in a more literal way, stepping out of the grey schist

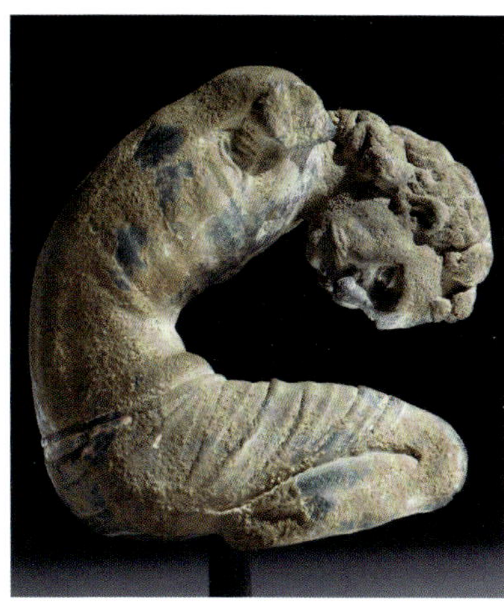

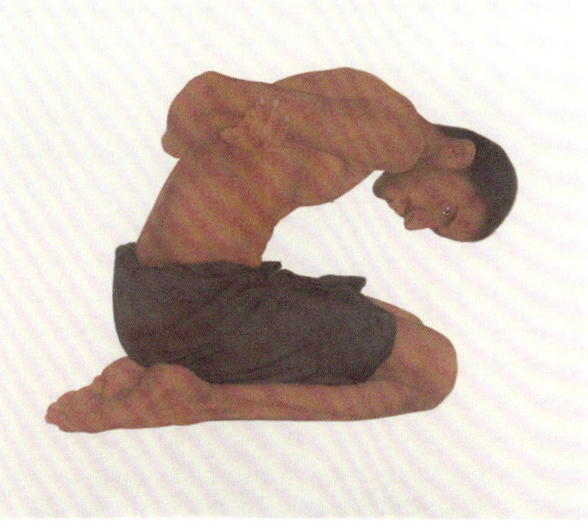

(left) Fragmentary figure of a mourner, Gandhara, 2nd–3rd century AD, schist, 11 x 11 x 7 cm
Ashmolean Museum, EA1999.33

(right) Ali Kazim, *Untitled (Mourner)*, 2020, watercolour pigment on paper, 70 x 114 cm
©Ali Kazim, courtesy Jhaveri Contemporary

sculpture into Kazim's version of the modern world. The figures become highly realistic in a manner reminiscent of his virtuosic contemporary portraits in watercolour. The kneeling figure of the mourner reflects Kazim's interest in people of faith. It is based on a fragmentary sculpture in the Ashmolean which is thought to come from a Gandharan scene of the *Parinirvana* - the death of the Buddha. Heedless of the Buddha's example of transcendent equanimity, this grieving disciple bows his head low in anguish, his distress conveyed by the exaggerated arc of the back. In Kazim's recreation, the mourner's arms are restored, clasped awkwardly behind his back like a prisoner's in a stress position. This ascetic, with his cropped hair and piercing gaze, is emotionally controlled but his thoughts are not clear.

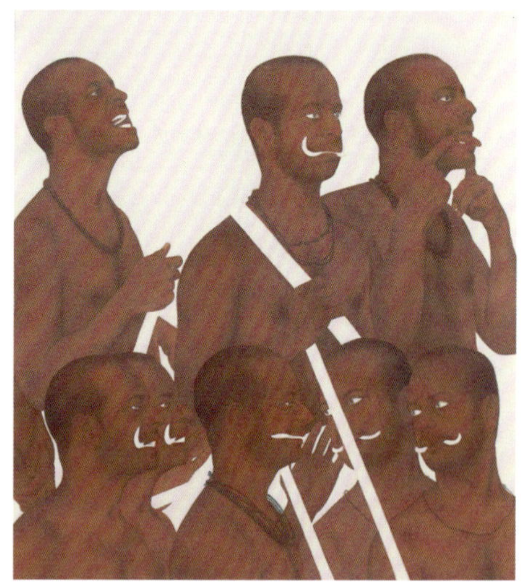

Ali Kazim, *Untitled (Mara's Army)* (detail) 2020, watercolour pigment on paper, 114 x 79 cm

Mara's Army depicts eight of the most monstrous humans imaginable. Its model is a famous Gandharan relief in Lahore Museum, which depicts the demonic followers of the Buddha's enemy, Mara, with bestial heads. In ancient representations of this scene, the snarling demons are almost comical, with their double faces or bared teeth. For all their captivating detail, they are not much more lifelike or frightening than medieval gargoyles. In Kazim's version, however, the creatures become flesh and blood: a band of close-shaven, bare-torsoed young men. All that remains of their demonic forms are the curling boar tusks protruding from the corners of their lips like ill-fitting dentures. They stare, or look at each other, or grimace tentatively. The luminously pale shafts of their weapons, the tusks and the whites of their beady eyes lend an eerie appearance to this enigmatic group, which in some ways is more intimidating than the Gandharan original.

In Kazim's work, the imagery of ancient Buddhism analysed by archaeologists merges with the artist's own personal iconography - the fund of ambiguous figures and forms with which he has experimented over the years. In *Mara's Army* and *Mourner*, the figures are no longer conventionally symbolic religious characters, to be decoded with expert knowledge; they have become humane, sentient, perhaps troubled people who attract us into their world.

ALI KAZIM

SUSPENDED IN TIME

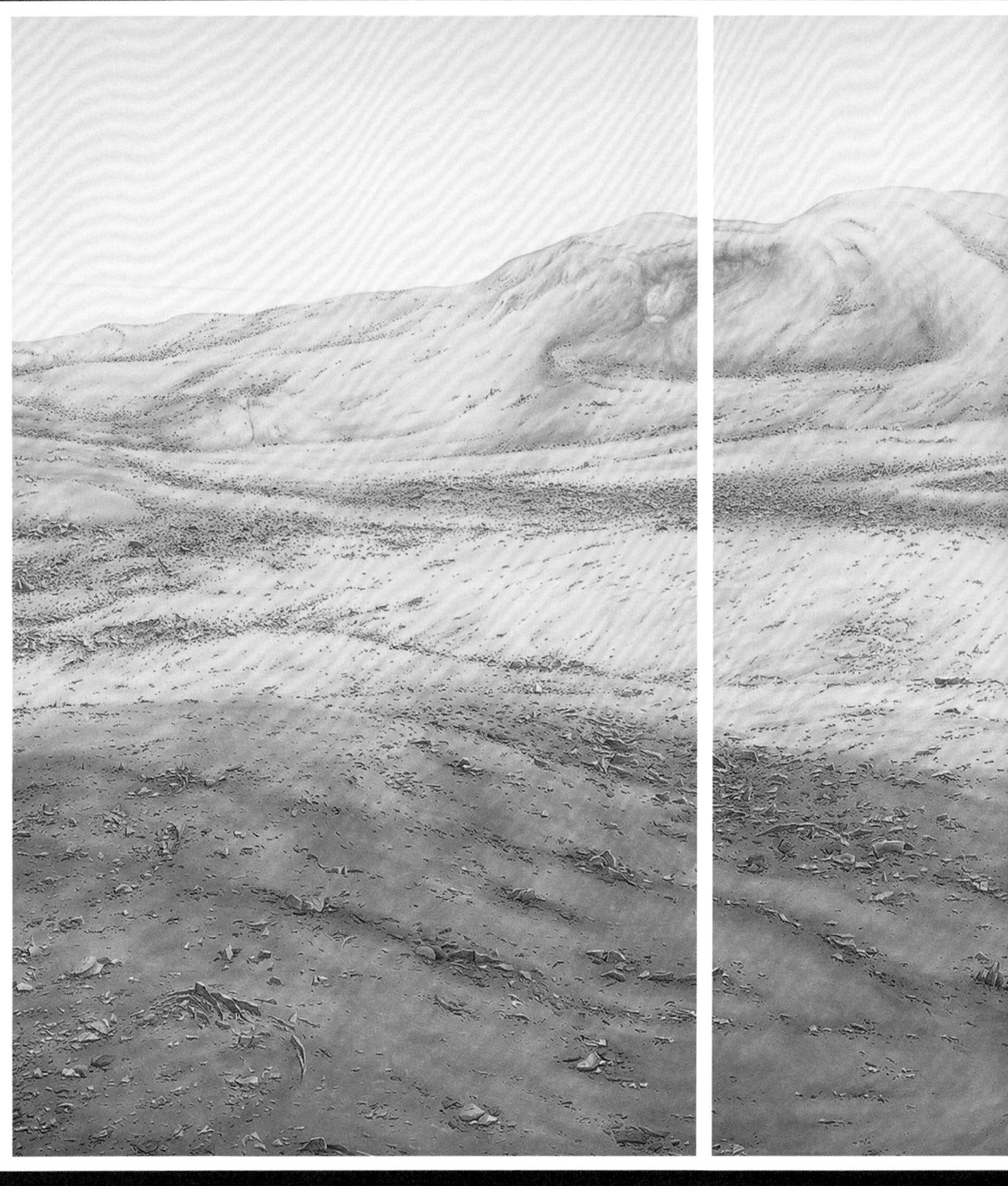

Ali Kazim, *Untitled (Ruins series, Triptych)*, 2018, watercolour pigment on paper, 193 x 358 cm

Collection of Sanda Lwin and Farhad Karim, ©Ali Kazim, courtesy Jhaveri Contemporary

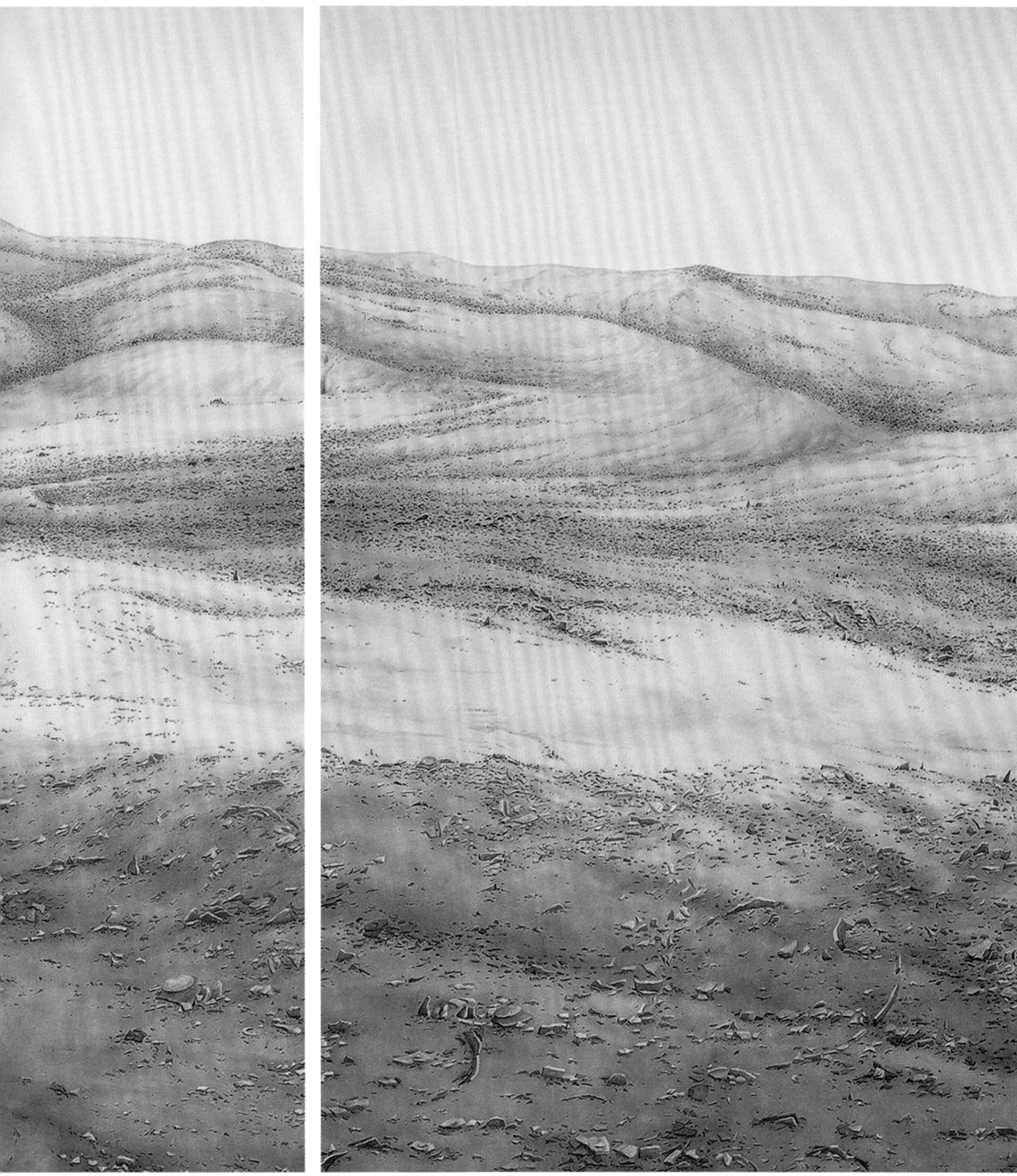

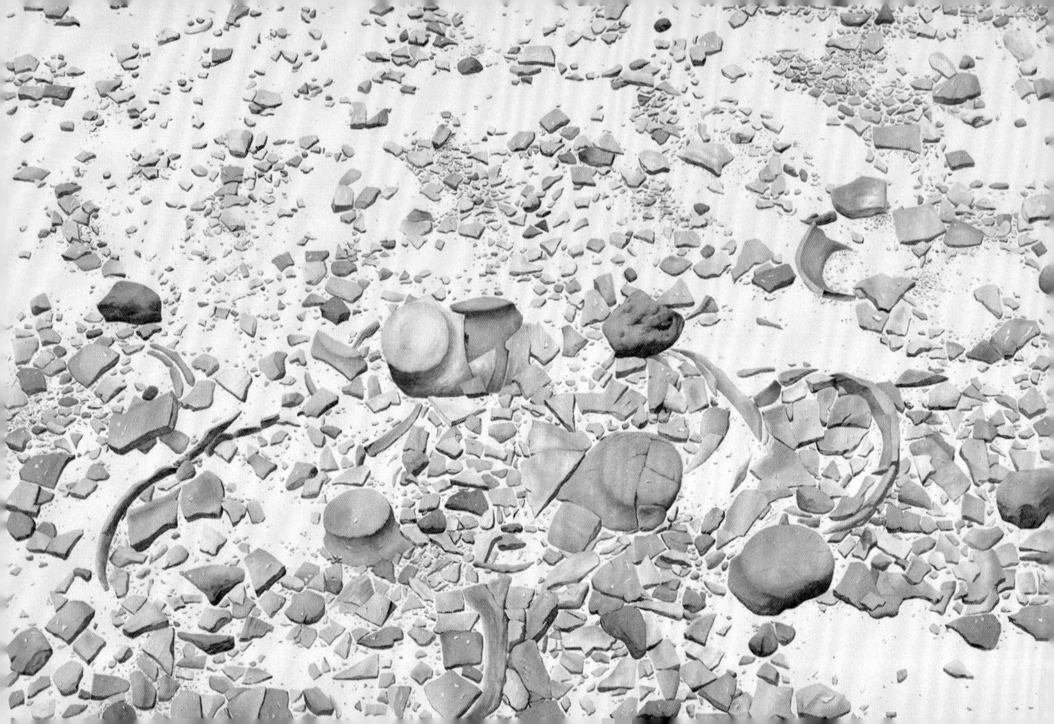

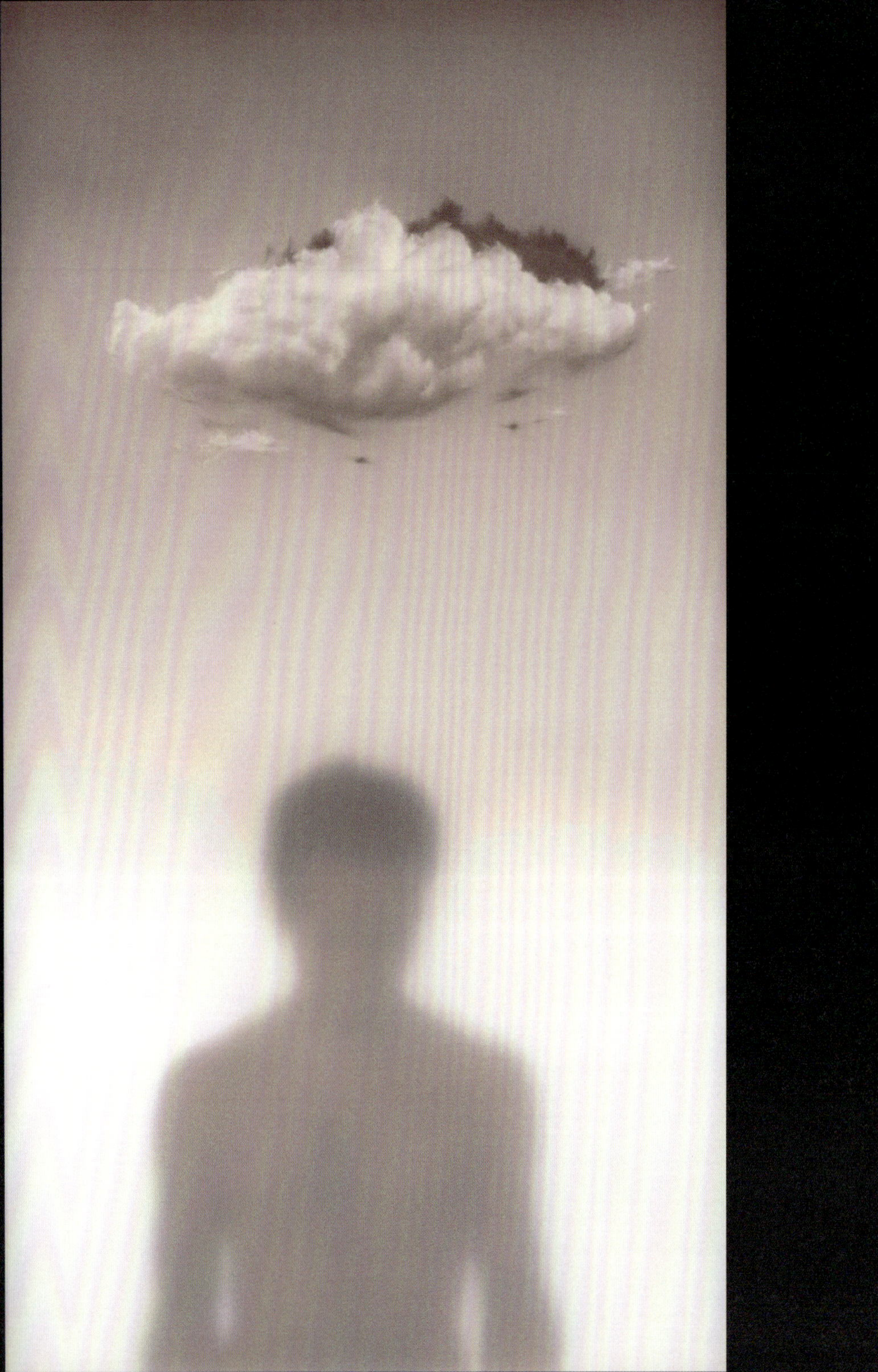

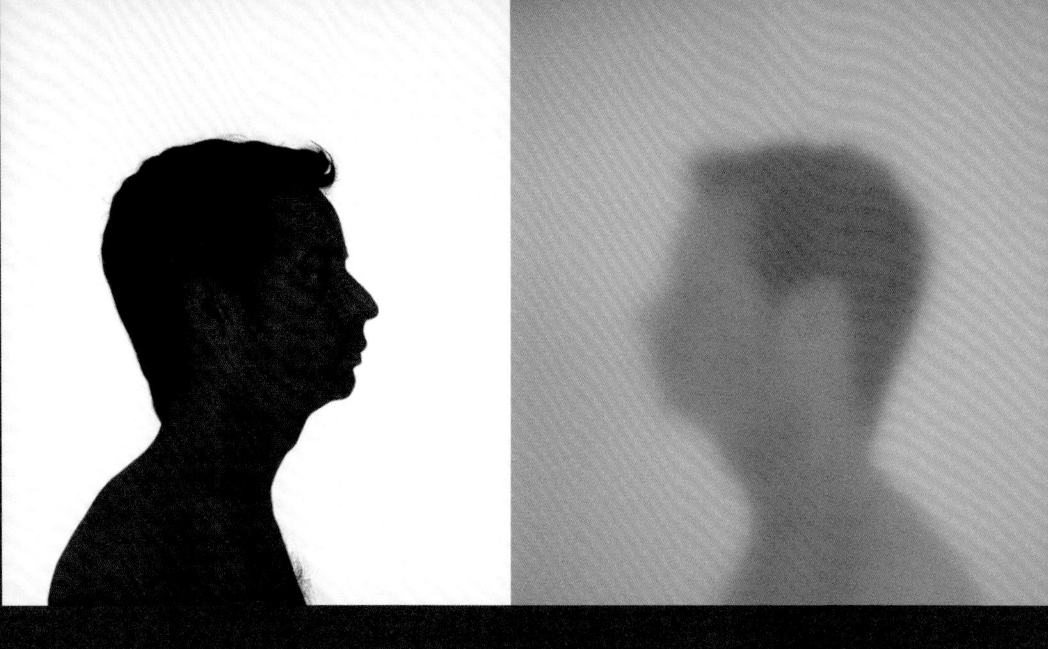

(opposite) Ali Kazim, *Untitled (Self-portrait with Cloud)*, 2014, watercolour pigment on paper and dry pigments on mylar, 68 x 40 cm
Collection of Taimur Hassan, ©Ali Kazim

(above) Ali Kazim, *Untitled (Self-portrait, diptych)*, 2012, watercolour pigment on paper and dry pigments on mylar, 45 x 78 cm
Collection of Taimur Hassan, ©Ali Kazim

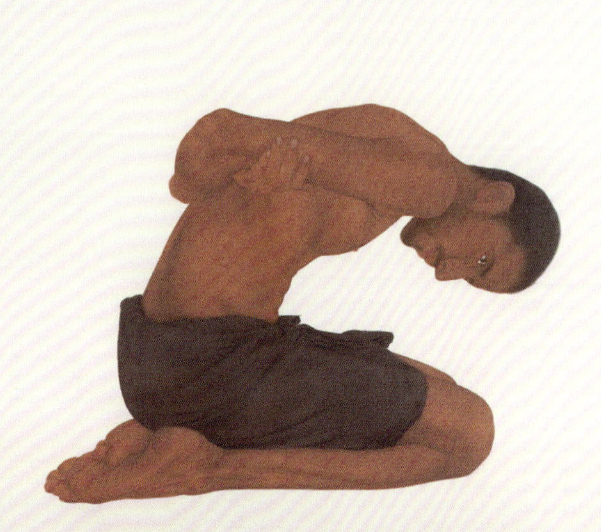

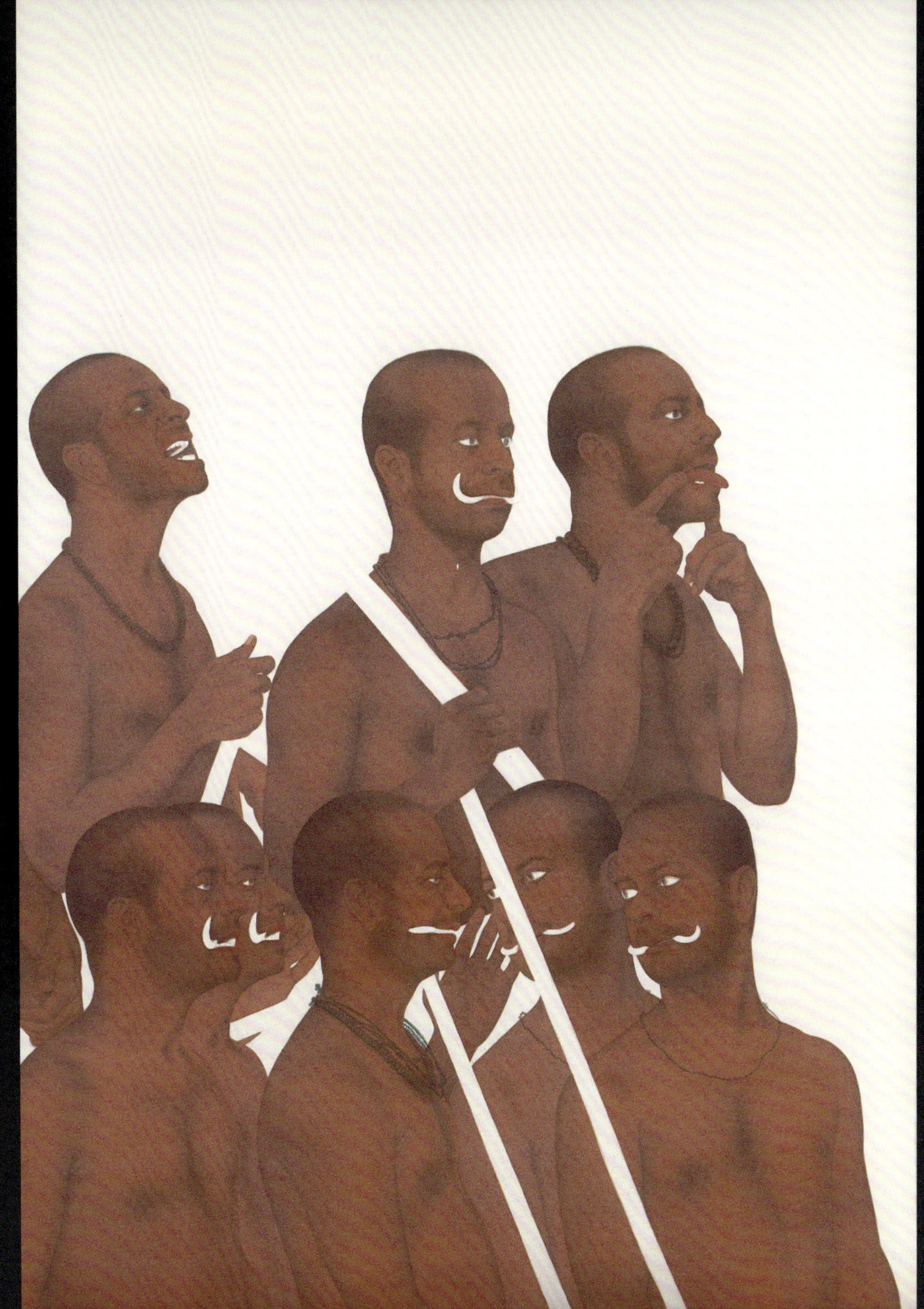

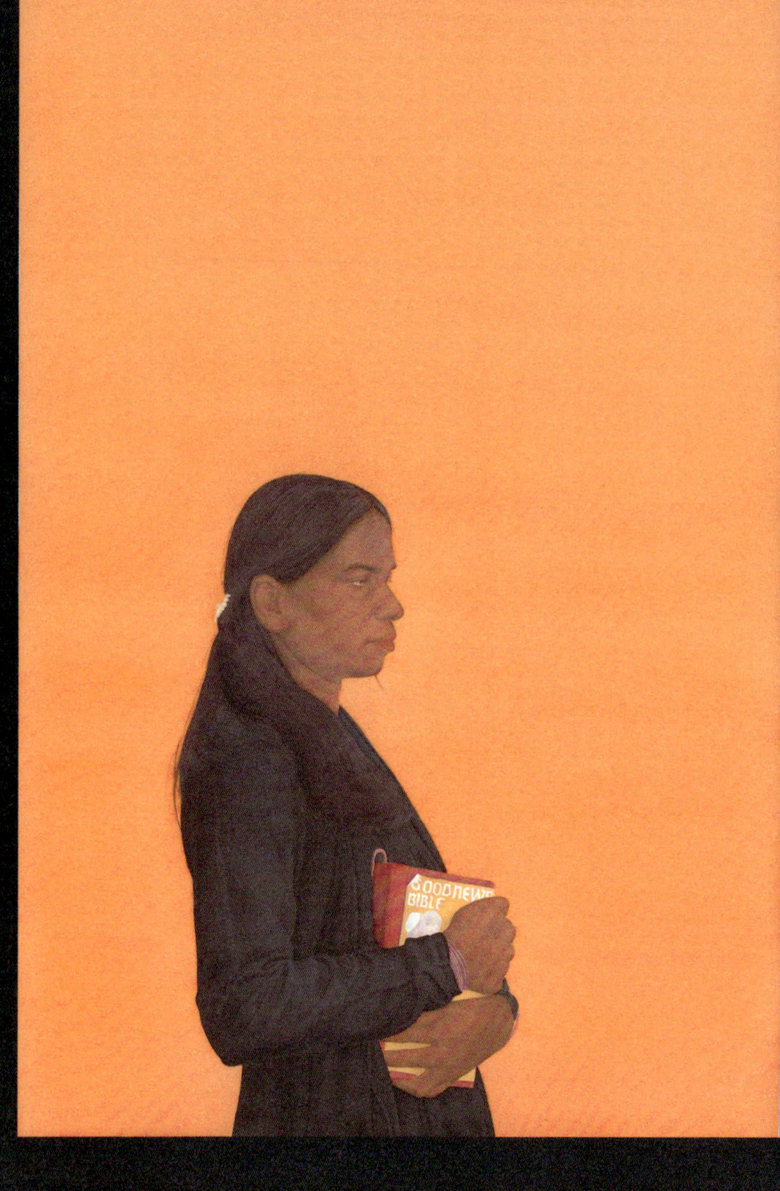

(above) Ali Kazim, *Untitled (Woman of Faith series)*, 2020, watercolour pigment on paper, 114 x 75 cm

(opposite) Ali Kazim, *Untitled (Man of Faith Series)*, 2019, watercolour pigment on paper, 71 x 56 cm

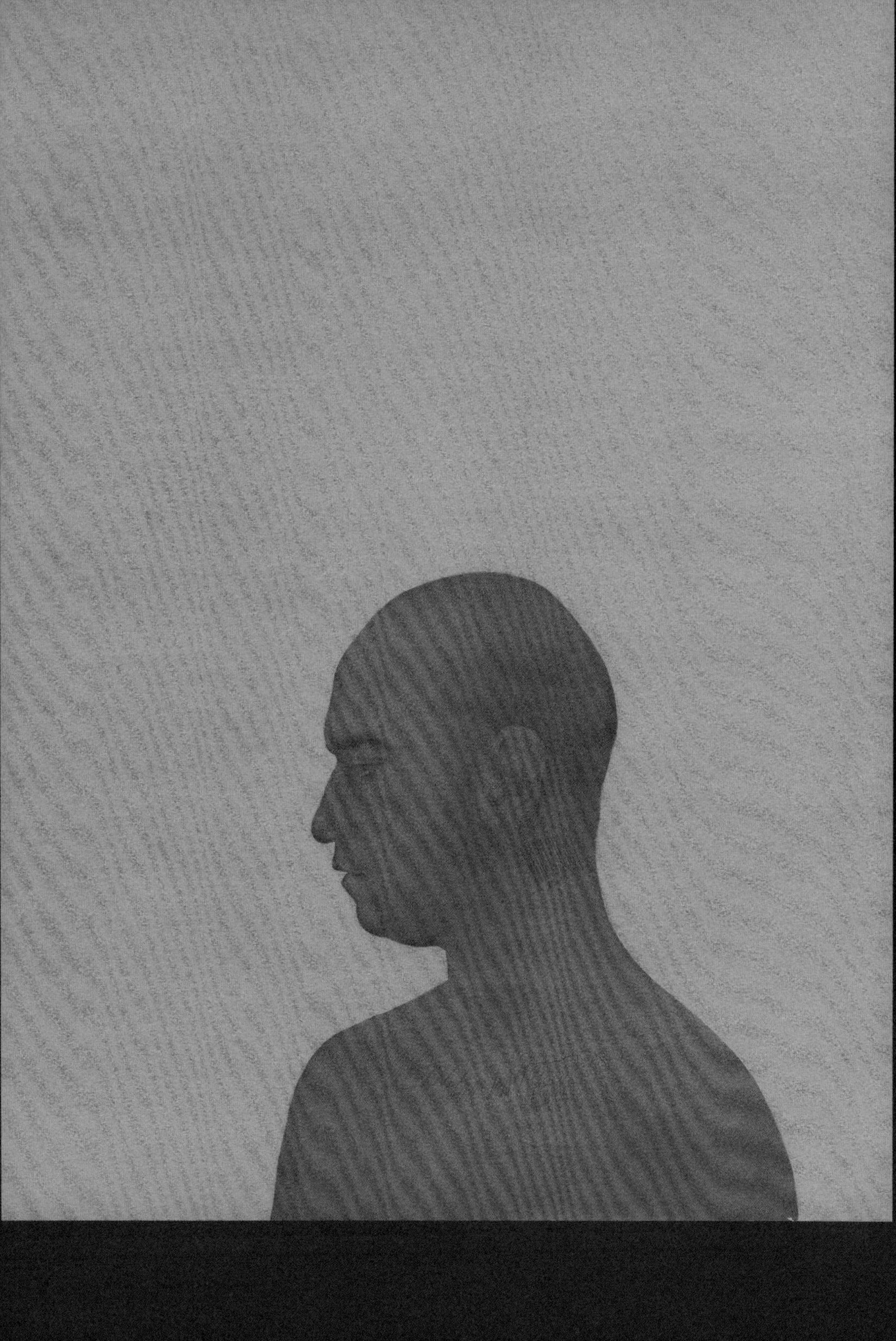

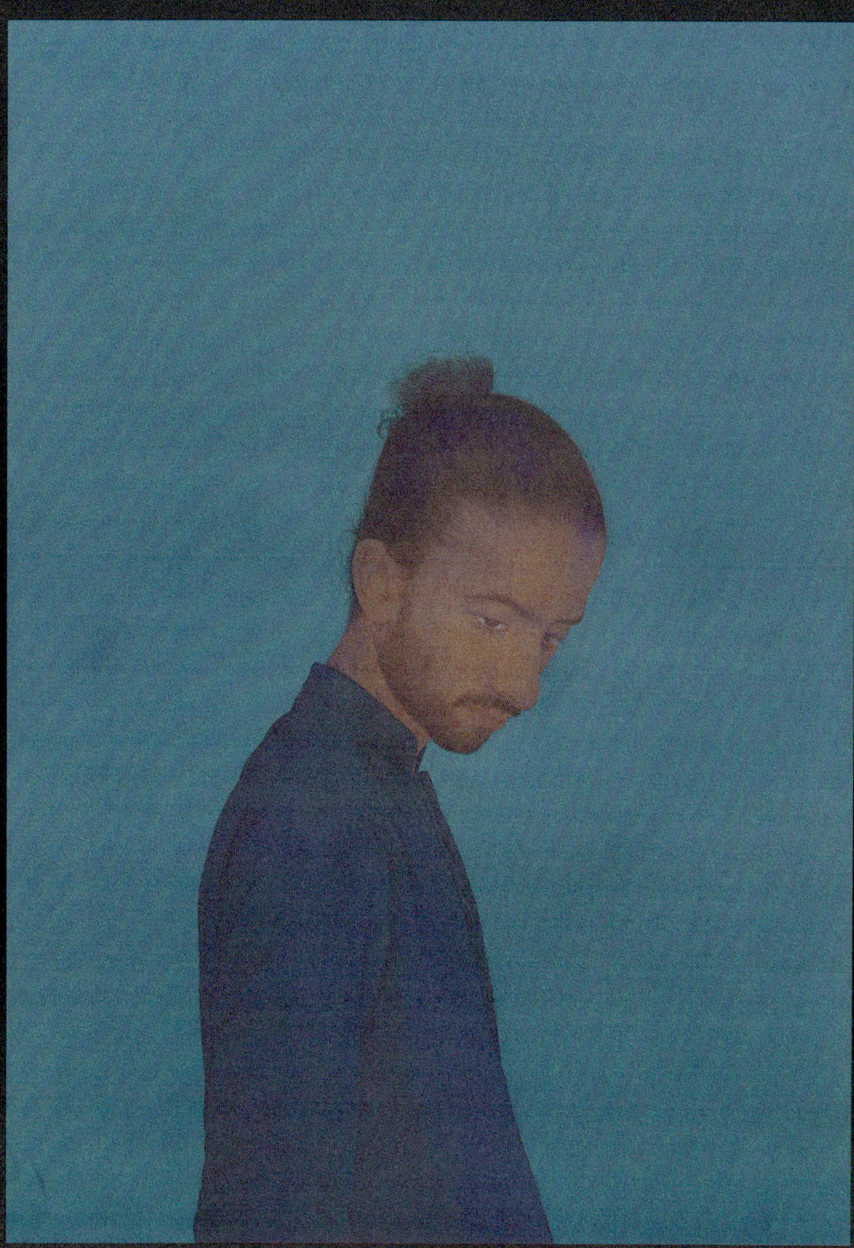

Ali Kazim, *Untitled (Man of Faith Series)*, 2020, watercolour pigment on paper, 62 x 44 cm

(opposite) Ali Kazim, *Untitled (Man of Faith Series)*, 2019, watercolour pigment on paper, 114 x 80 cm

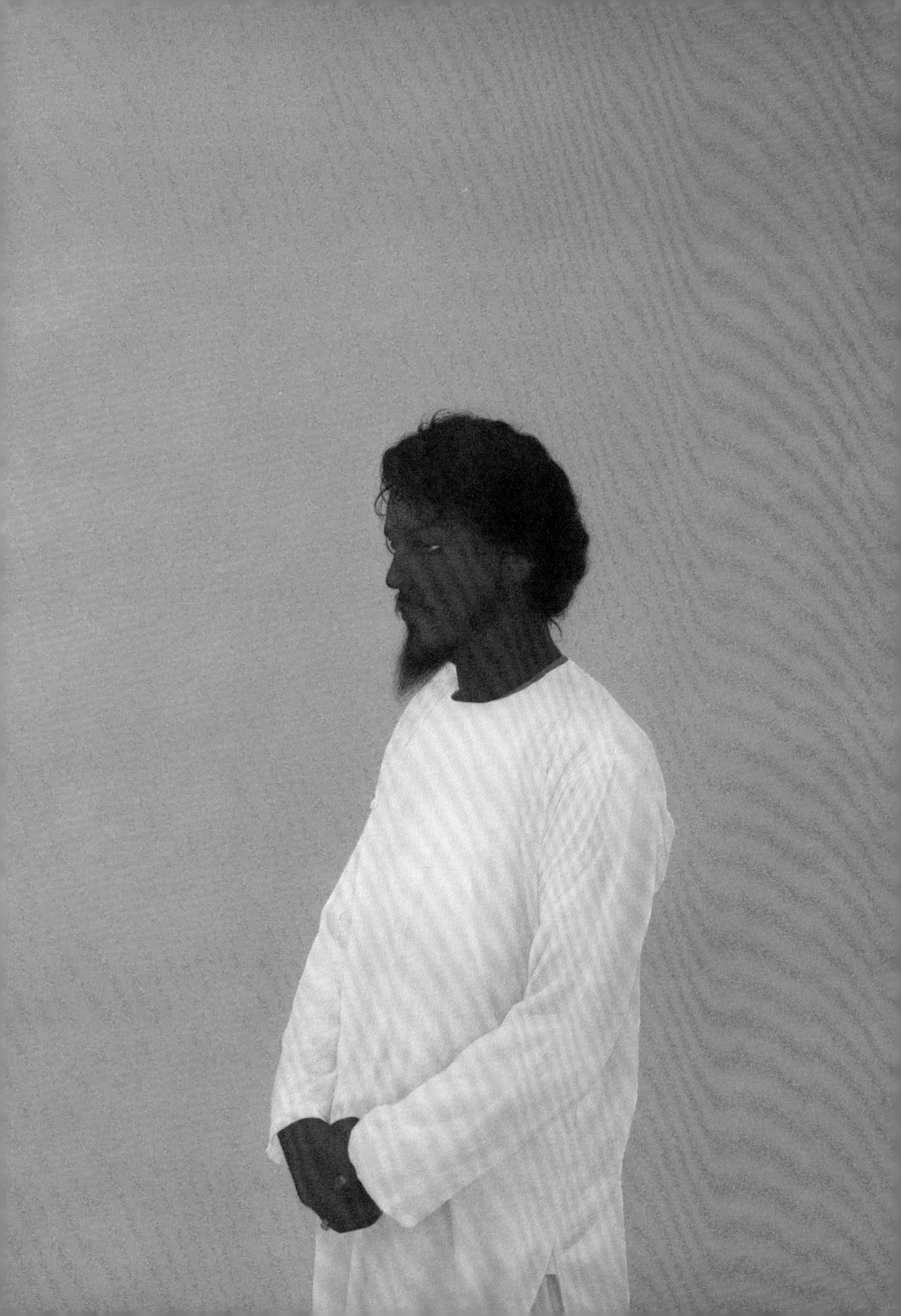

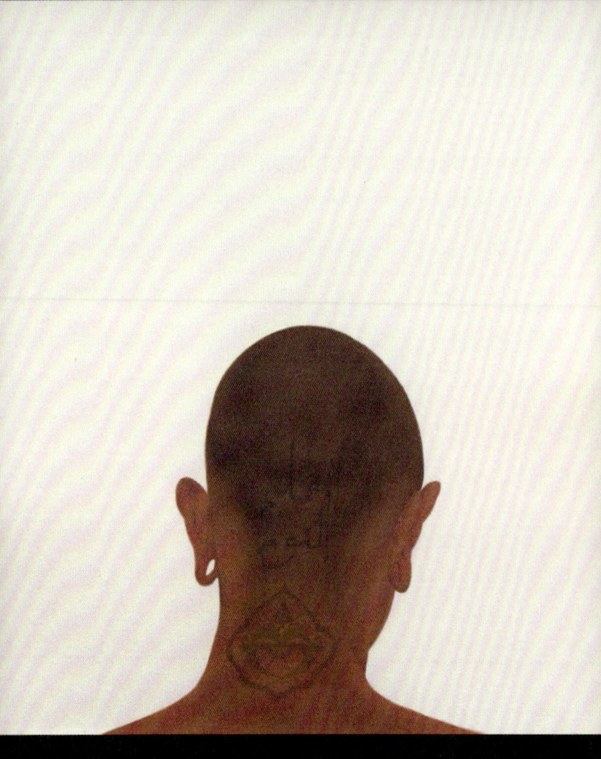

Ali Kazim, *Untitled (Man of Faith Series)*, 2019, watercolour pigment on paper, 56 x 46 cm

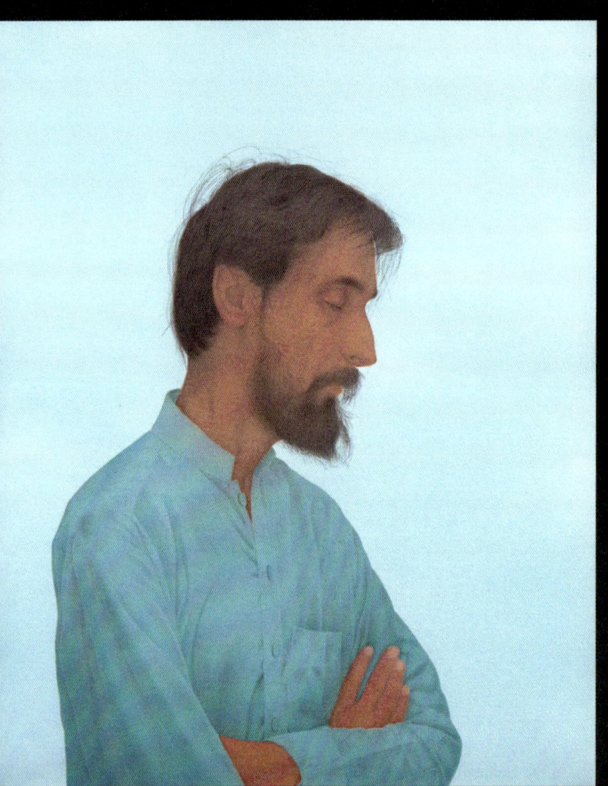

Ali Kazim, *Untitled (Man of Faith Series)*, 2019, watercolour pigment on paper, 56 x 46 cm

Colleciton of Tarika and Zafar Ahmadullah,

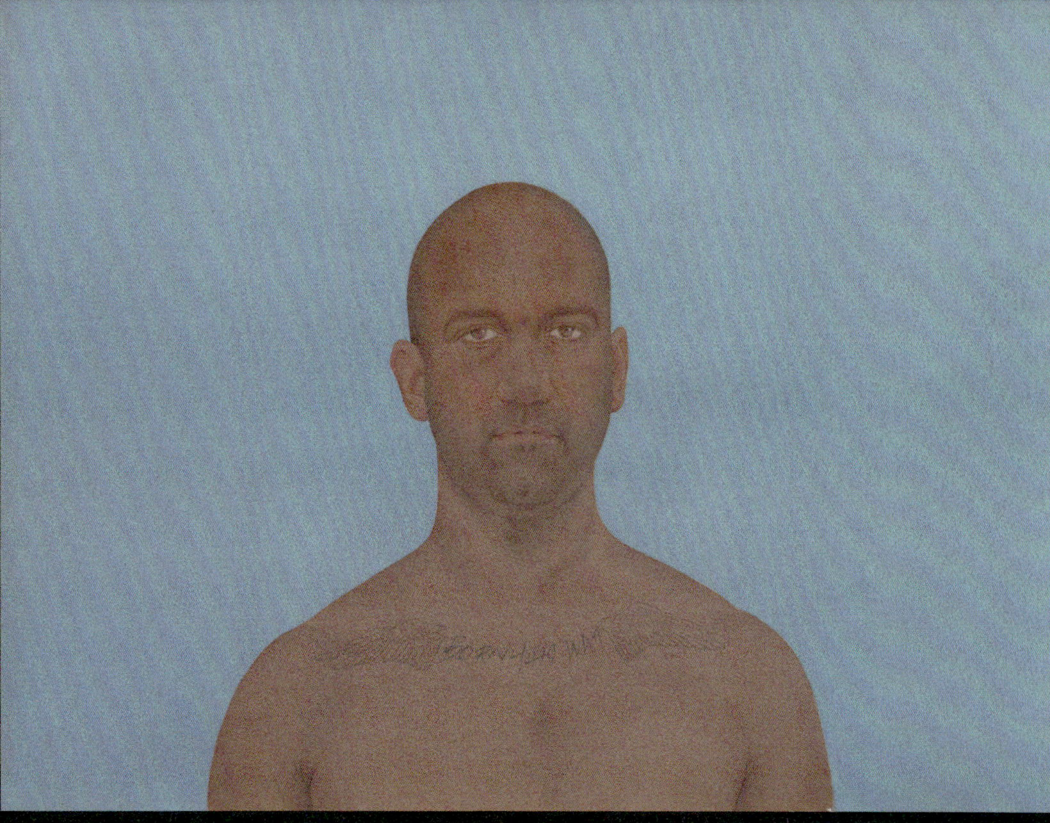

Ali Kazim, *Untitled (Man of Faith Series)*, 2020, watercolour pigment on paper, 50 x 67 cm

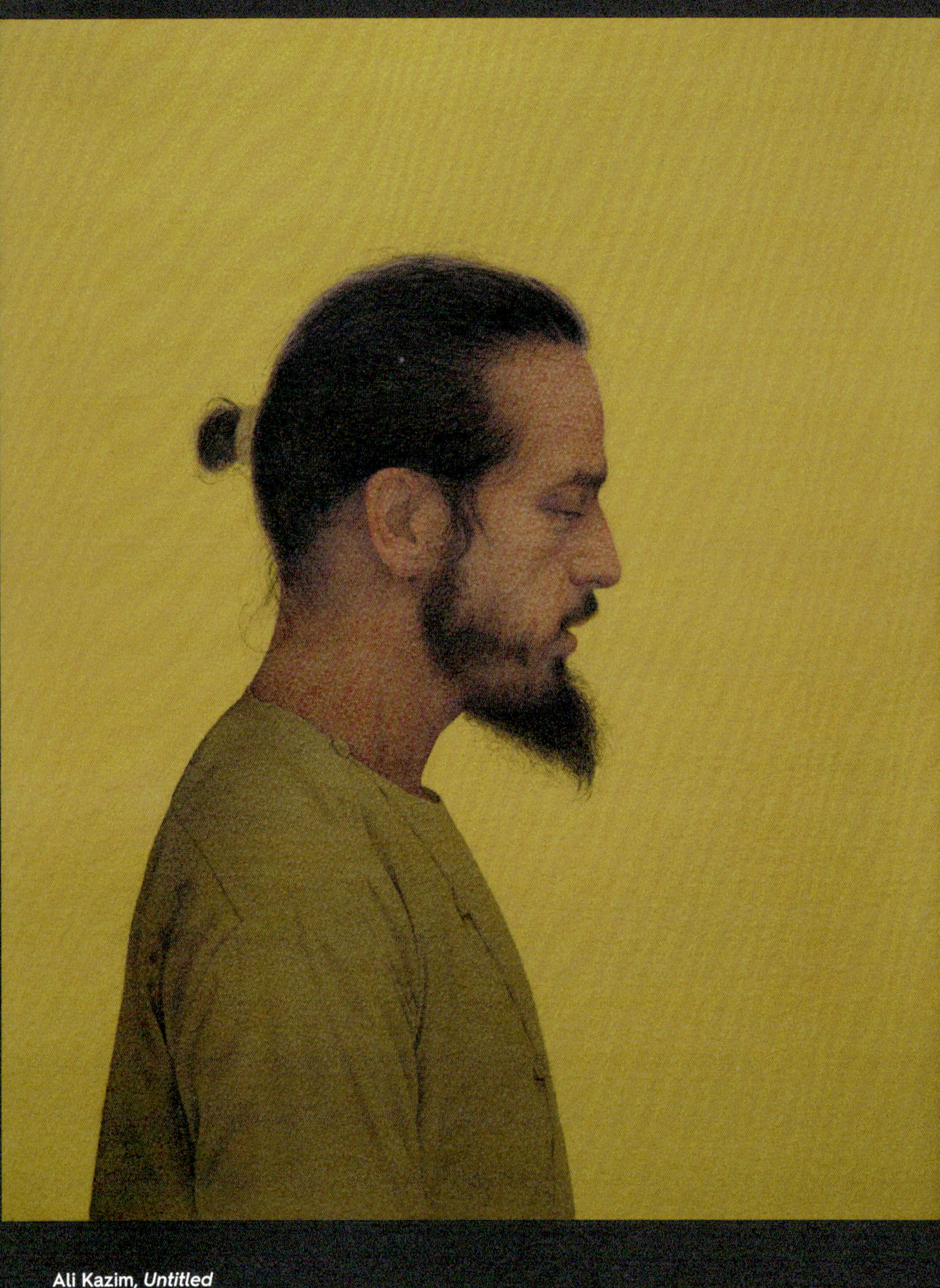

Ali Kazim, *Untitled (Man of Faith Series)*, 2021, watercolour pigment on paper, 42 x 34 cm

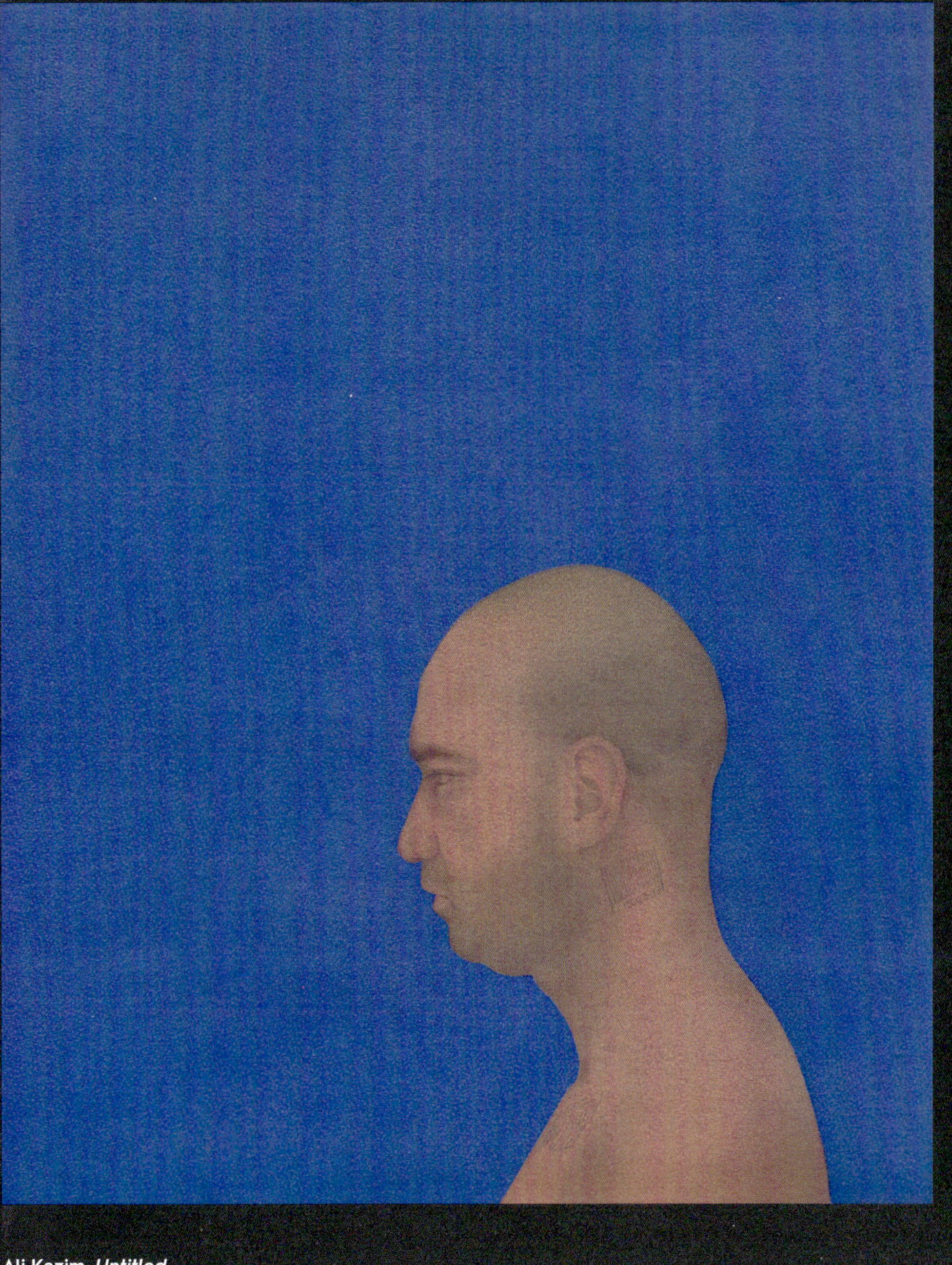

Ali Kazim, *Untitled (Man of Faith Series)*, 2019, watercolour pigment on paper, 71 x 56 cm

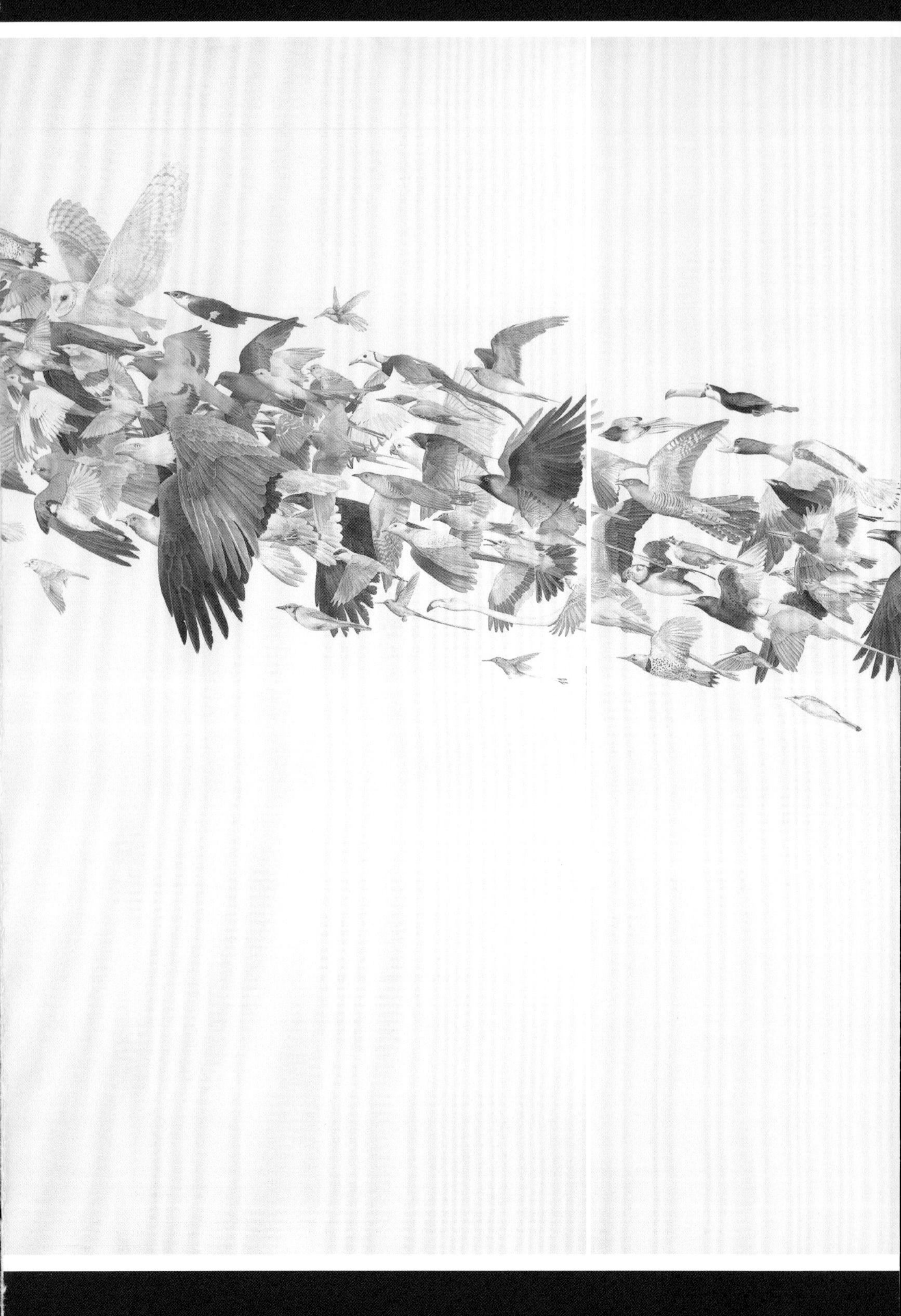

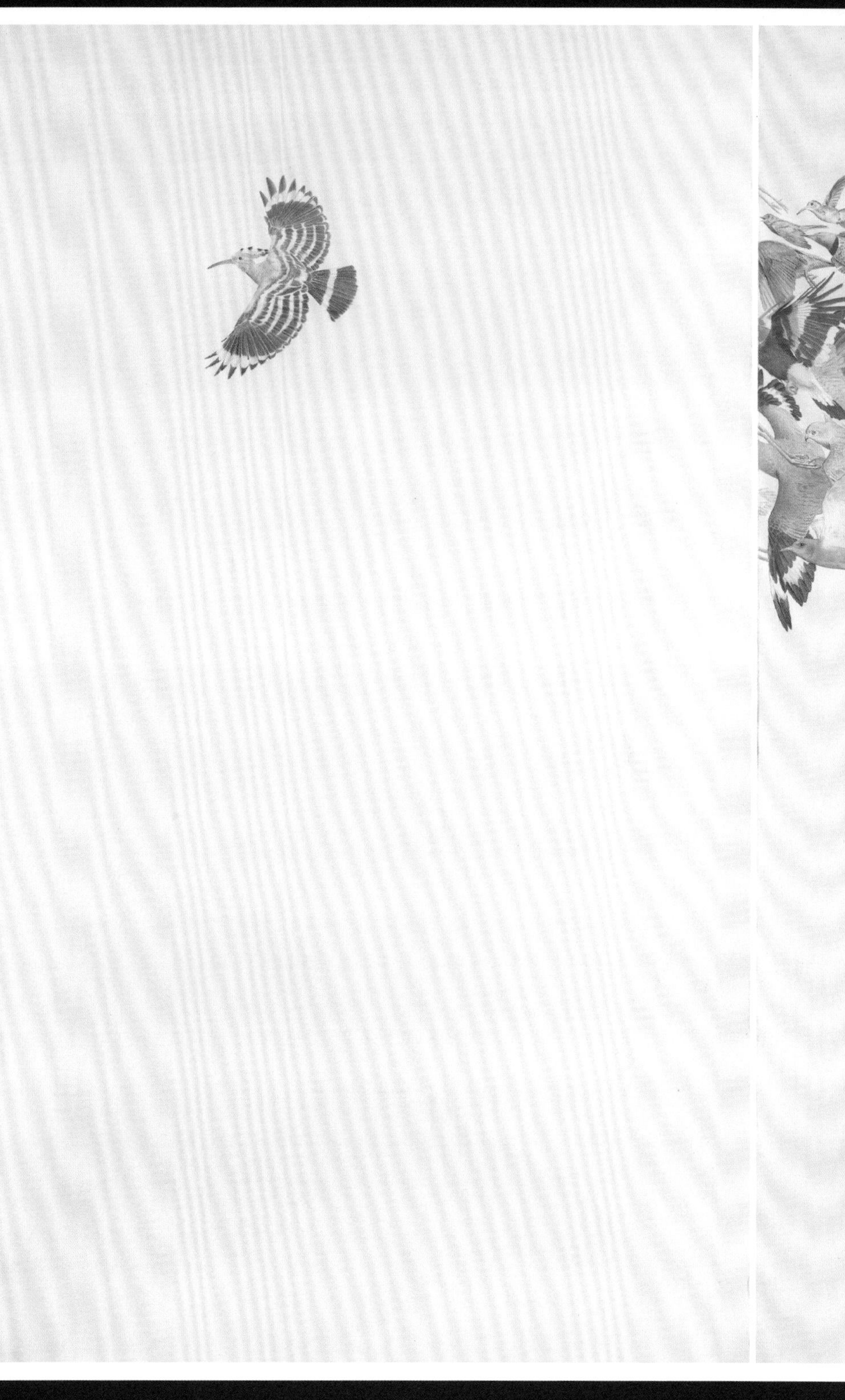

(overleaf) Ali Kazim,
Conference of Birds,
in 5 parts, 2019,
watercolour pigments
on paper, 198 x 570 cm

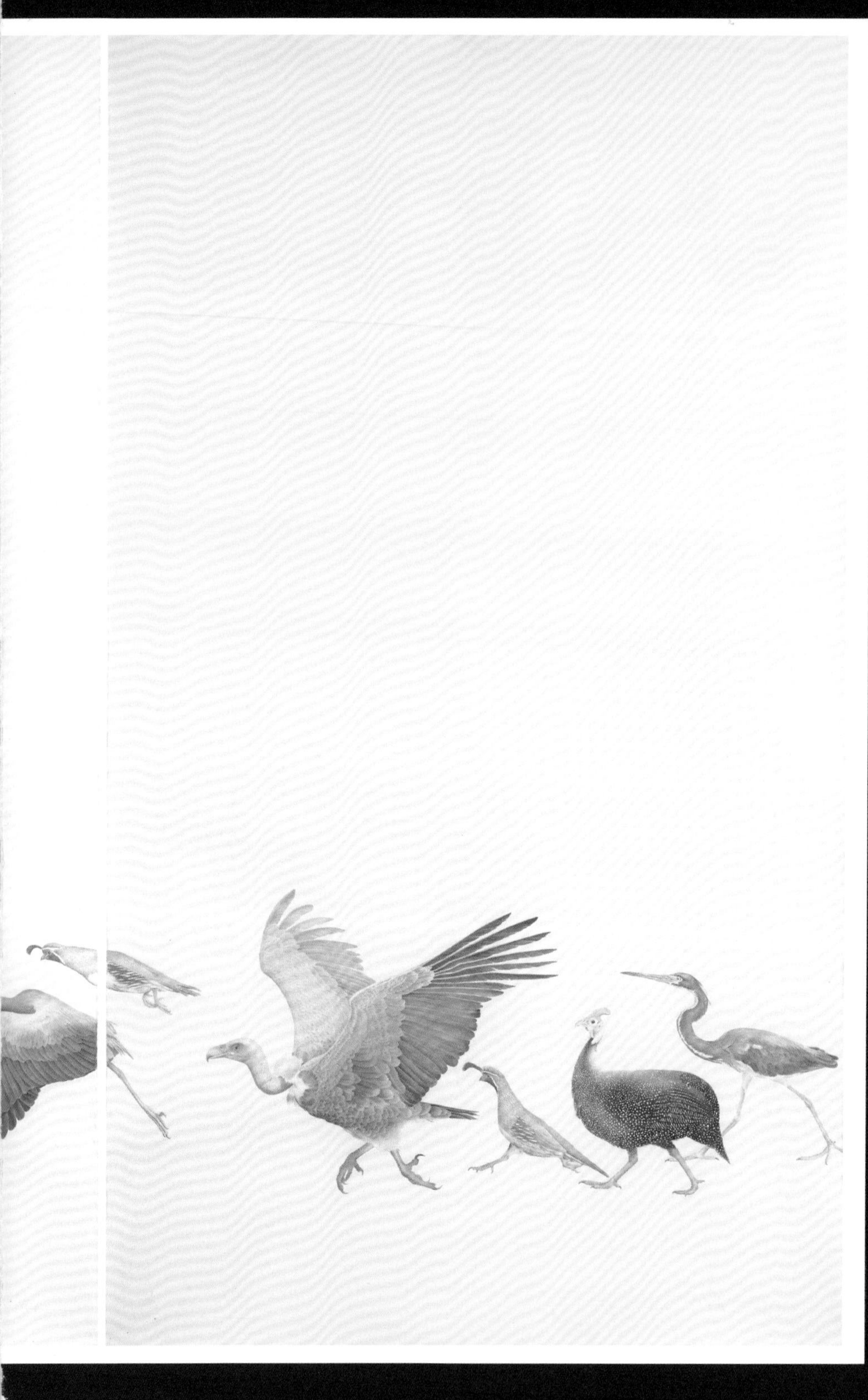

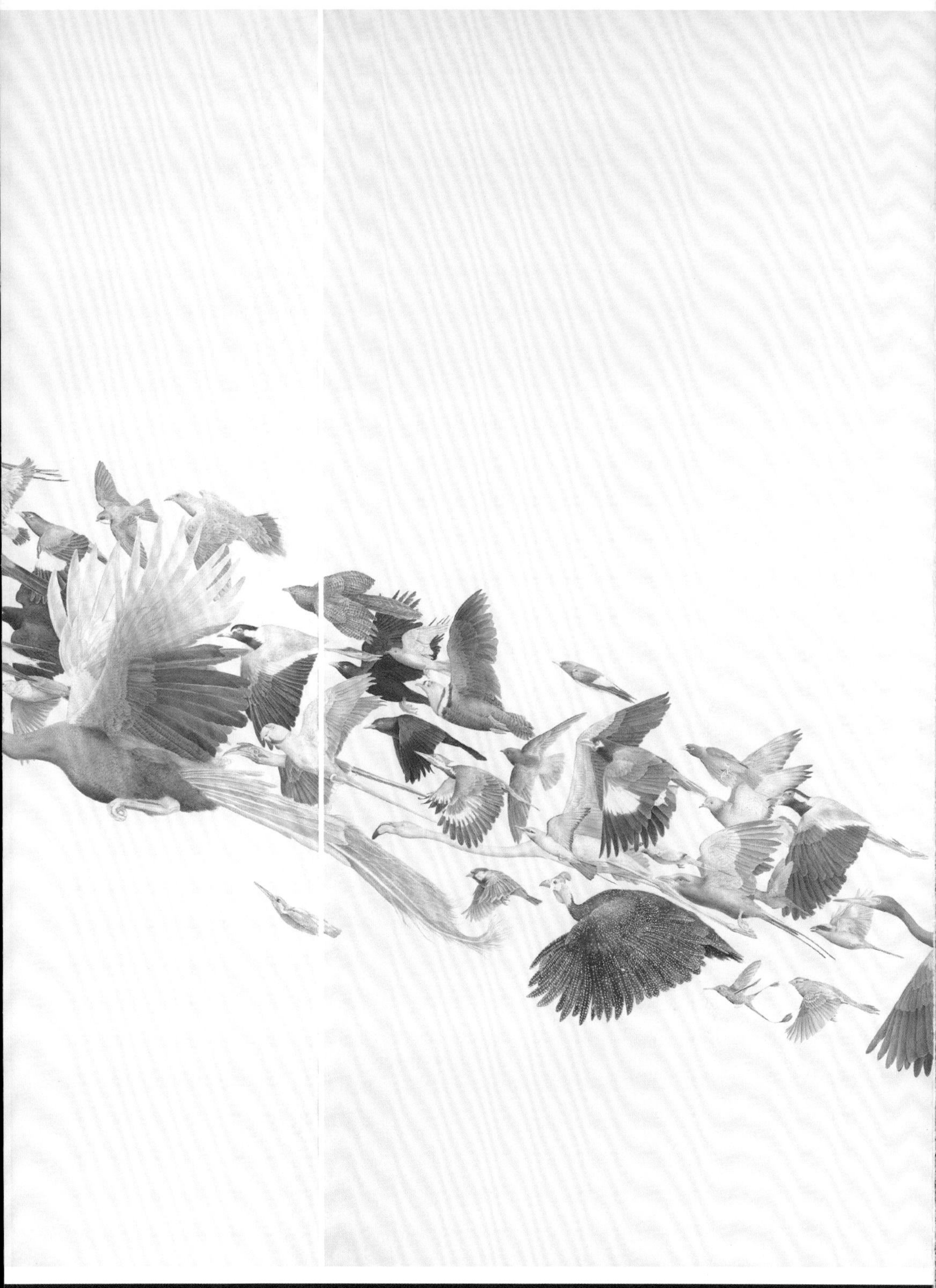

Ali Kazim, *Untitled (Bird Hunter III)*, 2020, watercolour pigment on paper, 72 x 86 cm

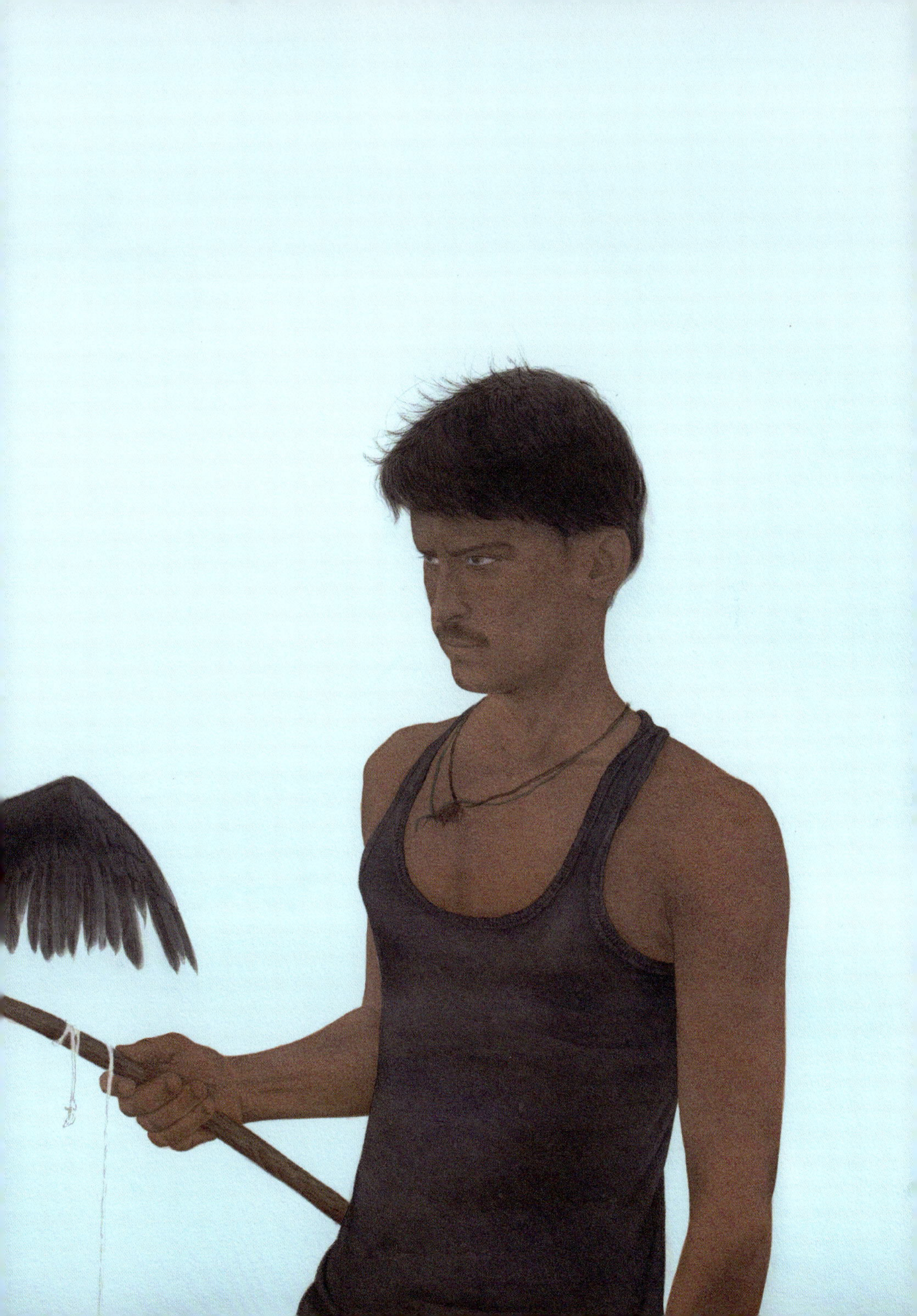

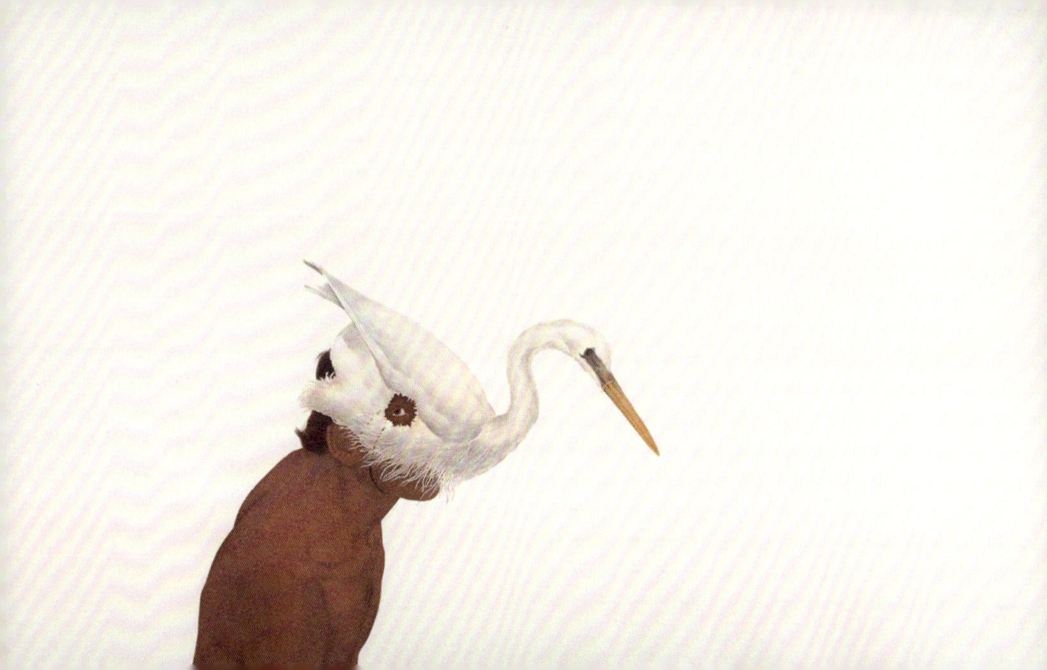

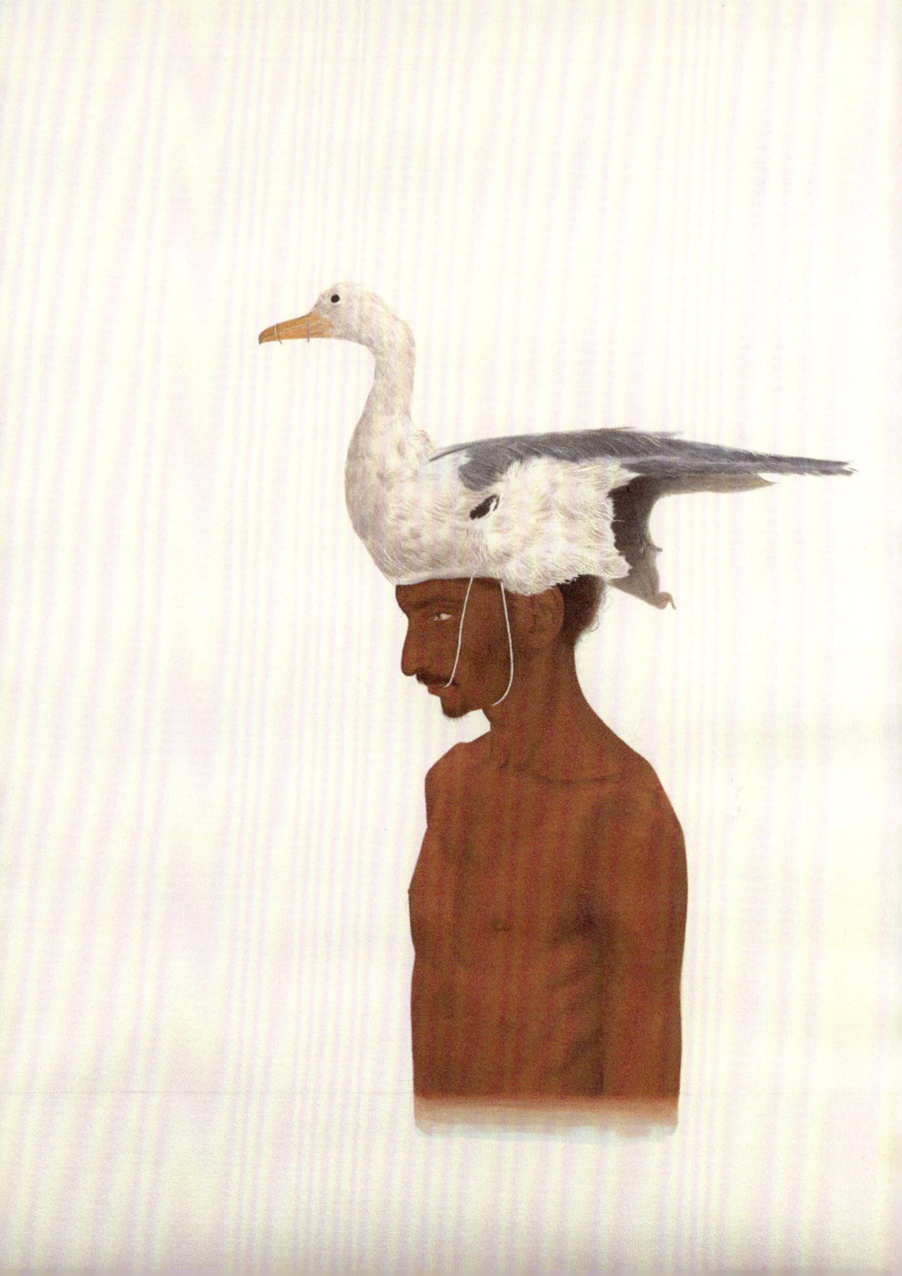

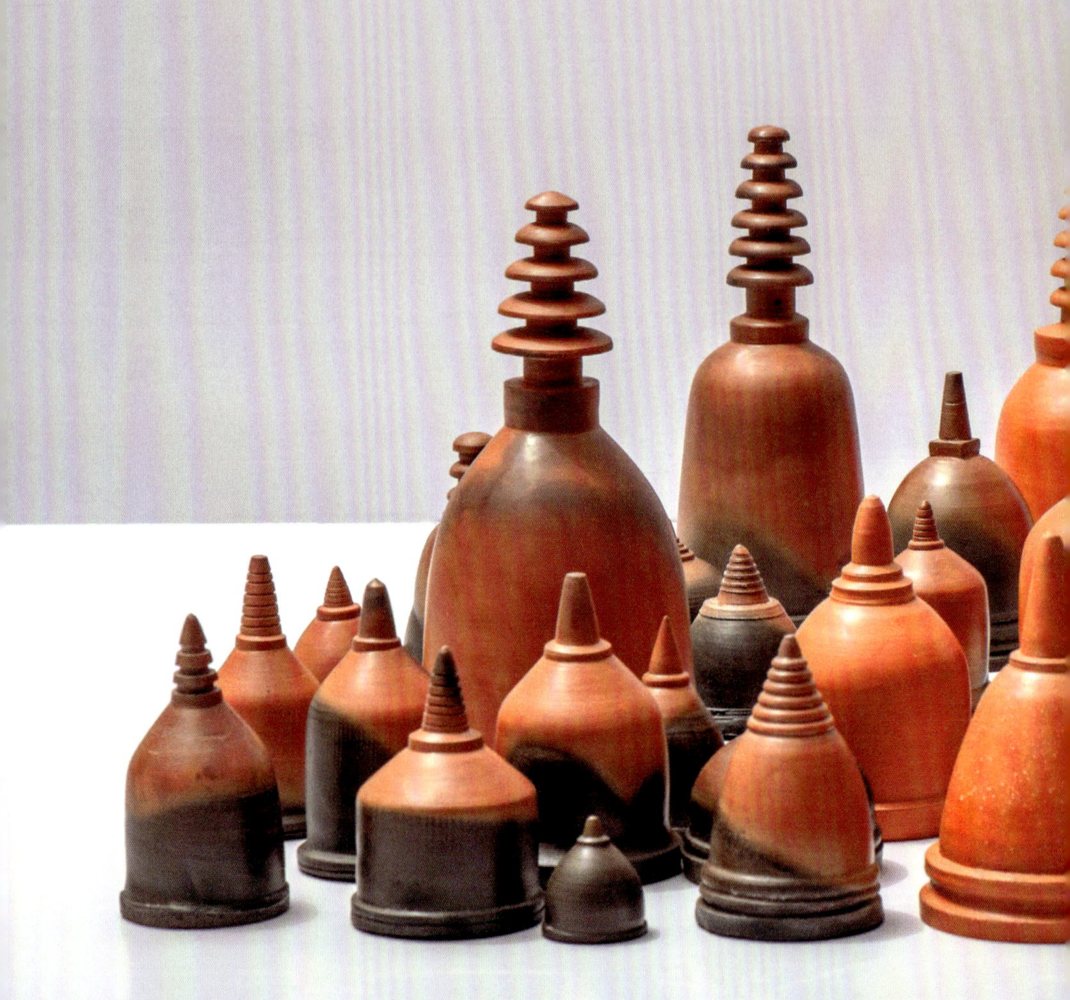

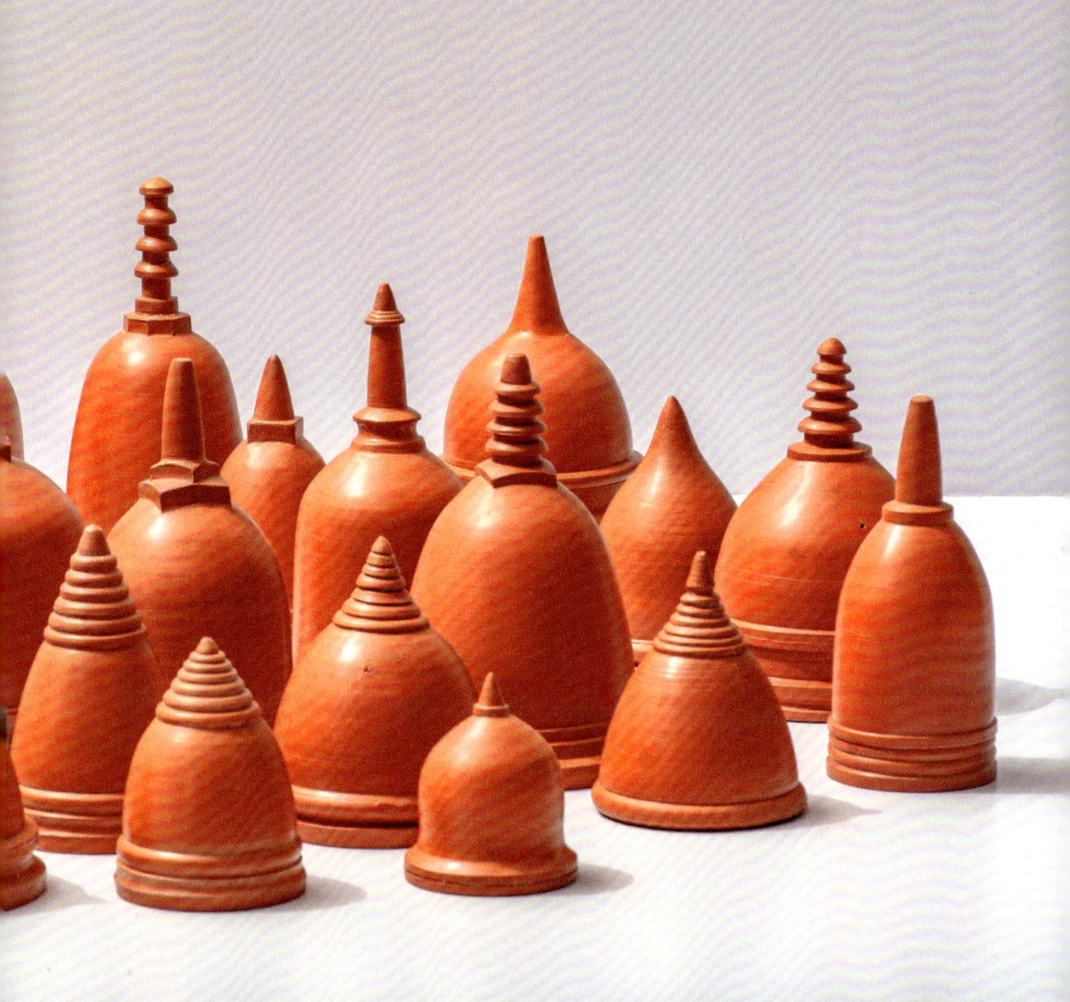

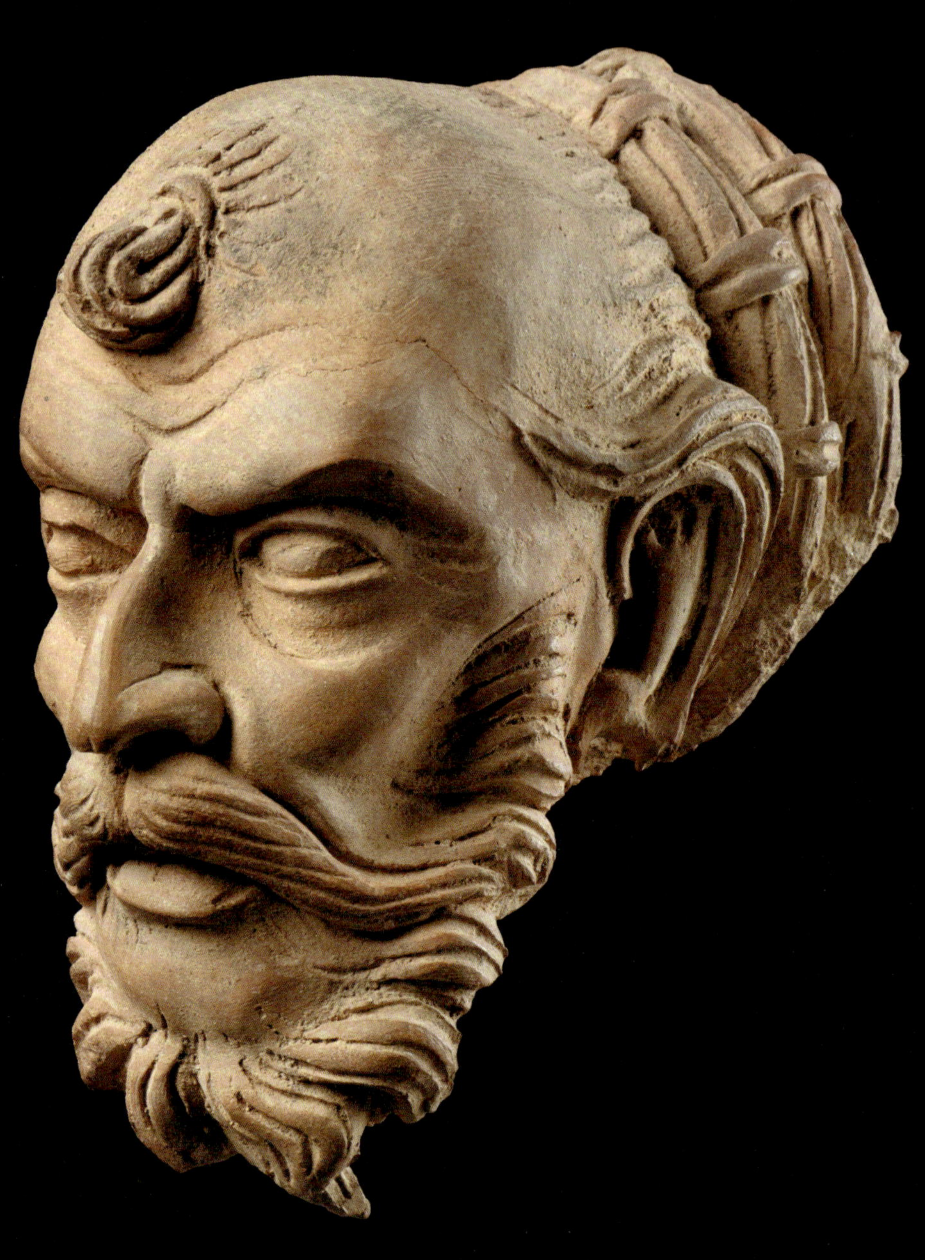

Chaitanya Sambrani and
Mallica Kumbera Landrus

PORTRAITS BEYOND SPACE AND TIME

ALI KAZIM'S PORTRAITS SET individuals against a uniform, unmodulated background of saturated colour, highlighting the figure with no extraneous detail. Kazim's long-standing study of Mughal and Rajput traditions of South Asian painting is evident here: portrait paintings in these traditions often concentrate on the subject to the near-exclusion of ancillary detail. His figures appear anonymous in their absolute presence, transcending specific location in place and time. They seem suspended beyond the immediacy of historical and geographic coordinates, and yet their cultural identity stands out. Produced through a process of close engagement with objects in the Ashmolean Museum, Kazim's paintings have a complex relationship with historical and geographical specificities. As a Pakistani-born artist studying objects of South Asian origin in a British museum, Kazim is attentive to the artistic traditions of the subcontinent, and to histories of trade and imperialism that underpin their institutional loci.

There is a grace about Kazim's subjects, who do not sit for the portraits. The individuals are often strangers, photographed on the street because they attract the artist's interest. Sometimes, Kazim might invite someone he knows to be photographed in his studio. He is uncomfortable working under the gaze of a sitter, or being pressured by the subject, and prefers to work alone, from photographs. For Kazim, it is the medium and the

Head of a Hindu ascetic, clay, unfired, 14.2 cm, Gandhara, c.301–400 AD
Ashmolean Museum, University of Oxford (EA1993.22)

colours that set the mood of the work, rather than the personality of the subject; however, details on the body of the figure do give clues to the identity, and sometimes faith, of the individual portrayed. Even as the impact of globalisation enables people to move and construct complex identities that can change depending on circumstances and conditions, Kazim remains fascinated with those elements of identity that individuals continue to hold close, and which help them make sense of who they are and where they come from.

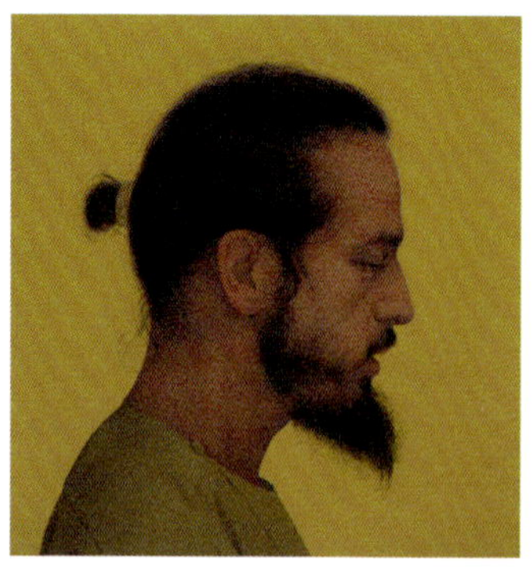

(above) Ali Kazim, *Untitled (Man of Faith series)* (detail), 2021, watercolour pigment on paper, 42 x 34 cm

Kazim's *Man of Faith* series employs an intense naturalism that characterises much of South Asian art, spanning a wide temporal and spatial span from Gandharan sculpture of the early centuries CE to provincial Mughal schools of the seventeenth and eighteenth centuries. This naturalism is discernible in close attention to detail: facial features, idiosyncrasies of bodily posture, details of uneven physiognomy - the kind of detail that tends to get evened out in idealised settings. Elements such as an unruly wisp of hair, an unevenly set mouth, or a peculiar twist of the neck assume expressive significance, offering glimpses into a latent narrative. Kazim tells us relatively little about these men, save that they are brown of skin and have facial features that could locate them in a broad arc from Afghanistan to Bangladesh. We are told, and perhaps believe, that these men have a deep sense of faith, which at first iteration we assume to be religious, and perhaps Muslim on the basis of their facial features. In all but one instance they gaze away from the viewer, as though in an intensely inward consideration of their appellation. Even in the one example where the gaze is directed outward, it is levelled *through* rather than *at* the viewer, signalling an intent beyond mundane appearances. The figures appear monumental against the background. Since they do not engage with their audience, the viewer can look closely (and without embarrassment) at the details of the delicate brush strokes in powder pigments. Using the Japanese wash technique, first introduced on the subcontinent in the early twentieth century through the pan-Asianist experiment of the Bengal School, Kazim makes the boundaries less distinct. The soft wash evokes an emotive quality, adding to the suggestion of a contemplative, solitary mood. Kazim compares the process of the washing of layers of paint to human ablutions: the ritual washing of the hands, feet and face required before prayer in Islam.

Kazim's *Man of Faith* series (and a solitary *Woman of Faith*) is *peopled* rather than populated: we are invited to meet distinct individuals and to contemplate their personal histories, uniquely shaped (as they must be) by their own experiences. In isolating their physical detail on unmodulated, monochrome backgrounds stripped of most, but not all, tell-tale context, Kazim gently insists that we contemplate their uniqueness and consider their profession of faith, with all the care that we would accord ourselves or those we hold dear. The works are universal and yet intimate - an invitation, even a petition, that we seek engagement with the latent narrative that underlies each individual visage. Each portrait is jewel-like in its minutely observed detail, set against a highly finished substrate that echoes the sophisticated process of preparing the *wasli*, a type of burnished, layered handmade paper used in South Asian miniature traditions.

Prior to 2019, Kazim's interests in examining exposed skin, membranes and blood vessels meant he explored mainly male figures. Kazim found his subjects in ordinary people: shirtless men working on the streets of Pakistan, known associates who could be photographed in the studio, and his own body. His works are introspective and his self-portraits, especially from 2014, engage with the space between the self and the divine using the veiled atmosphere of a nascent light. The unidentified space in this self-portrait is a bridge between man and sky, echoing inner expanses within the self. Like *Conference of Birds*, Kazim's portraits are an exploration of the spiritual inner self.

Ali Kazim, *Untitled (Self-portrait with cloud)*, 2014, watercolour pigment on paper and dry pigments on mylar, 68 x 40 cm
Collection of Taimur Hassan, ©Ali Kazim,

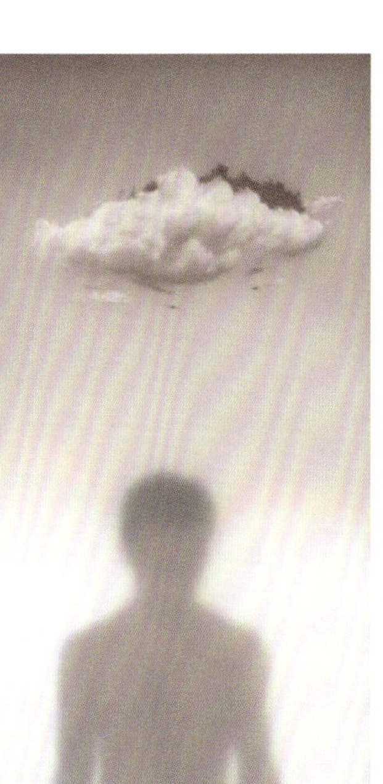

> *'We shall not cease from exploration*
> *And the end of all our exploring*
> *Will be to arrive where we started*
> *And know the place for the first time.'*
> - T S Eliot

While many of his past subjects were strangers photographed on the streets of Pakistan, and the emphasis on bare skin made men the obvious subjects of his work, more recently the focus of Kazim's interest has moved from skin to identity. His subjects now appear draped in kurtas, pyjamas and vests. The start of his *Woman of Faith* series illustrates a female subject who carries a book in her hands. On closer examination, the book is the holy

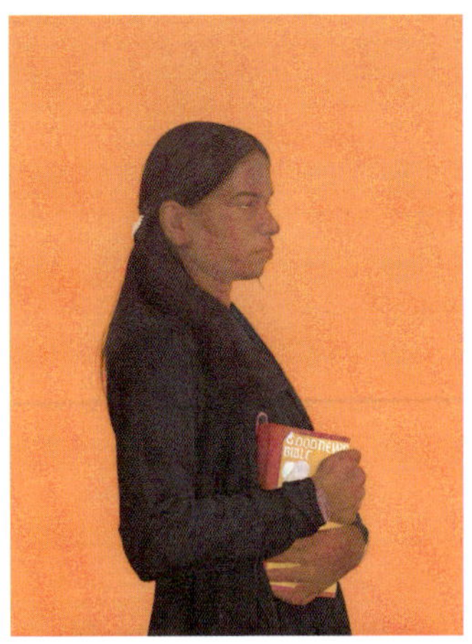

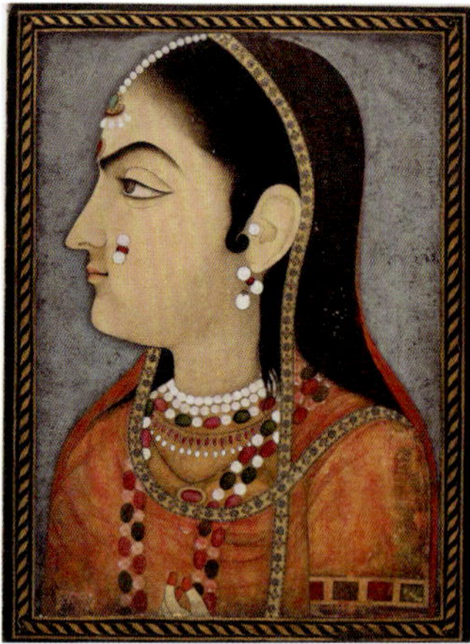

(left) Ali Kazim, *Untitled (Woman of Faith series)*, 2020, watercolour pigment on paper, 114 x 75 cm
©Ali Kazim, courtesy Jhaveri Contemporary

(right) Portrait of a lady, gouache with gold on paper, 31.5 x 23.8 cm, Jaipur, India, *c*.1800
Ashmolean Museum, University of Oxford (EA1967.162)

bible. Such paintings resonate with the spirituality Kazim finds imbued in Sufi poetry and Buddhist sculptures, which he has suggested continue to manifest their original devotional purpose.

Following Kazim's study of a diverse range of works (from Indus, Gandharan, Persian, Mughal, Rajput and Deccani traditions) in the Ashmolean collections come intriguing paintings that pick out and accentuate arresting idiosyncrasies the seeds of which are often discernible in some detail of posture or expression in historical works. Kazim continues to deploy his highly polished, monochrome grounds as inscrutable *mise-en-scene* for a drama that has no immediately recognisable narrative. The *Bird Hunter* series of three paintings play with expectations of what relationships may exist between the human and avian characters. In two instances we are led to imagine a drama of the hunt, where obsessive pursuit produces a surrealist melding of the hunter and the hunted. Presented in a starkly reduced palette dominated by whites and browns, the visage of the hunter-seeker is enveloped and transformed by (into) the body of the quarry. The third work in the series invites speculation on relationships surrounding servitude and domesticity: the dark-skinned man gazes fixedly at the captive cormorant at the end of his stick, the latter spreading out its wings in impossible flight against an azure ground that both mimics and exceeds the blueness of a clear sky.

Of the 2020 works, *Untitled - Mourner* and *Untitled - Mara's Army* make the clearest reference to historical objects from Gandhara: the first is a fragmentary figure from the Ashmolean's collection that could be held in the palm of a hand; the second is a sculptural slab found near Peshawar in northwest Pakistan, now in the Lahore Museum.

In the first work, the schist figure of a male mourner, kneeling and bent over in visceral agony, is transformed by Kazim into an exercise in re-enactment, the one visible eye strangely turned halfway towards the viewer. Re-enactment makes a more overt appearance in the second work, where Kazim uses self-portraiture to engage with a key episode in Buddhist mythology, animating the gestures and expressions of the demonic soldiers of Mara's army, who essay forth to deter the meditating Bodhisattva Gautama as he nears the final realisation of Enlightenment and Buddha-hood. Amplifying geometrical resonance through graphic symmetry and repetition, Kazim picks out and accentuates the wonder and delight of the Peshawar army of Mara. The figure of Mara appears as the force of delusion in Buddhist mythology. The sculptor(s) of the Peshawar slab depict the forces of delusion as a horde of human-animal hybrids, a practice of imaginative delight discernible in many Asian and European representations of demonic (and sometimes divine) entities. Modelled on Kazim's own face, the figures in his painting seem to play at being demons, as though trying out and comparing notes on ways of being fiendish.

Kazim's representational oeuvre extends beyond his figurative paintings into atmospheric landscapes and ruins. He is excited by finding imprints of a potter's hand or fingers on ancient sherds and other terracotta material. He calls these powerful moments of 'time-travelling', and credits a key moment in his artistic development to his experiments with clay. He is fascinated by surface finds like terracotta sherds and artificial topographical features such as mounds or a 'tell' – signs of accumulated remnants; of organic and cultural refuse; of collapsed mudbrick buildings of generations of people who once dwelt on the same site. While these pictures are not peopled, Kazim calls them 'portraits of past communities'. For Kazim, the sherds are physical memories of people who shaped the clay with their fingers, leaving imprints for future generations to find. The landscape is a mirror which allows those looking at – or touching – surface finds to confront the past and reflect on the present.

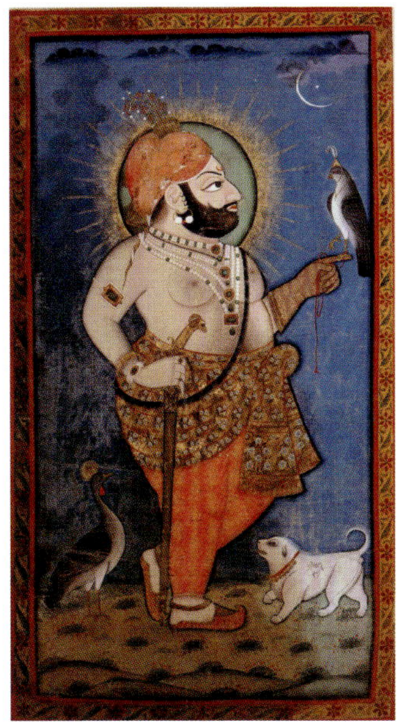

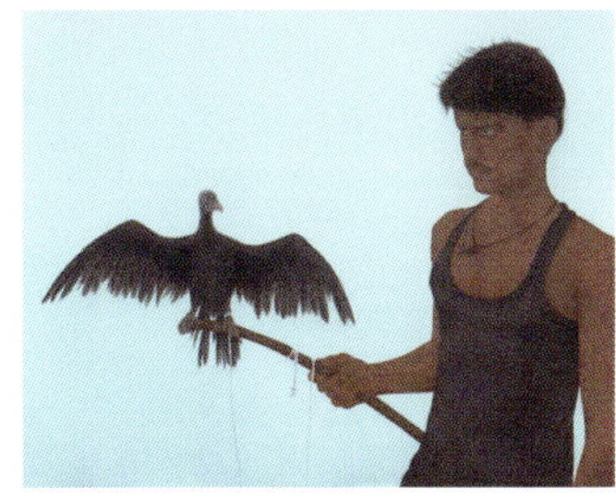

(top) Maharana Bhim Singh with a hawk, gouache with gold on cotton cloth, 107 x 59 cm, Udaipur, India, 1805–1810
Ashmolean Museum, University of Oxford (EA1985.31)

(above) Ali Kazim, *Untitled (Bird Hunter III)*, 2020, watercolour pigment on paper, 72 x 86 cm
©Ali Kazim, courtesy Jhaveri Contemporary

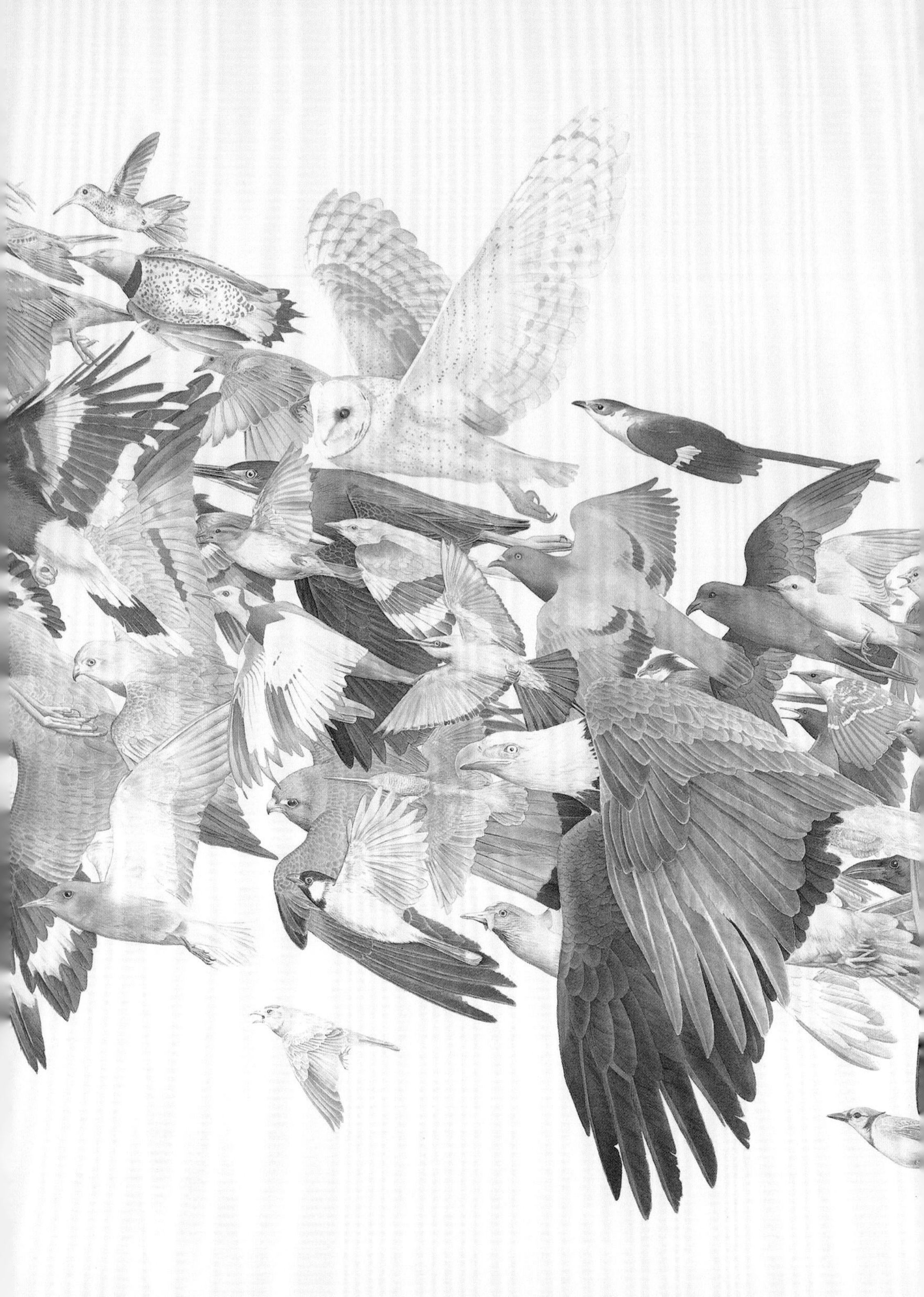

Francesca Leoni and
Mallica Kumbera Landrus

THE CONFERENCE OF THE BIRDS AND ITS ARTISTIC LEGACY

FEW WORKS OF PERSIAN LITERATURE have inspired the visual arts across Asia more than Farid al-Din 'Attar's *Mantiq al-tayr*, literally 'the language of the bird' or, as it is best known, 'the conference of the birds'. From fifteenth century illustrated manuscripts to contemporary artworks, the tale of these God-seeking creatures inspired a wide range of visual adaptations and interpretations, immortalising the poem's characters and message.

Completed around 1177 in the city of Nishapur, in northeastern Iran, the *Mantiq al-tayr* is an allegorical poem framed by a story within which shorter tales and parables are told. The main narrative describes the long and perilous journey of a group of birds in search of their king, the Simurgh. In their quest they are led by the hoopoe, 'the courier of every valley' and Solomon's trustworthy messenger, who convinces them to abandon the transient and temporary constraints of their present existence in favour of greater rewards:

'If you desire this quest, give up your soul
And make our Sovereign's court your only goal.
First wash your hands of life if you would say:
"I am a pilgrim of our Sovereign's Way";
Renounce your soul for love; He you pursue
Will sacrifice his inmost soul for you.'
– 'Attar 1984, lines 730-735.

Ali Kazim, *Conference of Birds, in 5 parts* (detail), 2019, watercolour pigments on paper, 198 x 570 cm
©Ali Kazim, courtesy Jhaveri Contemporary

Seven valleys separate the travellers from their king's abode on Mount Kaf. Each tests their motivation and resilience, but also reflect the steps they need to take to reach their final goal. The first is the valley of the quest, where all beliefs, true and false, are cast aside; the second is the valley of love, where reason is abandoned; the third is the valley of knowledge, where the travellers realise the uselessness of worldly experiences; the fourth is the valley of detachment, where mundane attachments are left behind; the fifth is the valley of unity, where the birds realise that everything is connected; the sixth is the valley of wonderment, where all previous assumptions are shattered; and finally, the seventh is the valley of poverty and annihilation, where by transcendence the self becomes one with the universe.

During the trip many birds succumb - some to thirst and illness, others to attacks by beasts, or to fear. In the end, 30 birds reach the coveted destination, only to recognise their own image in their king. The Persian word *sīmurgh*, in fact, consists of the terms *sī* - 30 - and *murgh* - bird - a cunning poetic hack that distils the story's morals into a single word. The journey towards the Simurgh is thus one of self-discovery: by finding their king the birds, in fact, find their true selves.

The journey of these birds has yet a higher spiritual meaning in Islamic societies. The journey symbolises the experience of the soul yearning to become one with God, a concept central to Sufism, or Islamic mysticism. Like the birds, Sufis follow the guidance of an older master (known as *pir* or *shaykh*) and embark on a path of transformation that eventually leads to unity with the Godhead. Although 'Attar is not known to have been a Sufi, his exposure to Sufism at the peak of its development - and to contemporary masters such as Majd al-Din Baghdadi (d.1219), one of the deputies of the Kubrawiyya order - helps to explain the intensely mystical inspiration of his works (Lewihsohn, 1999). Indeed, along with two other Persian masters - Sana'i (d.1131) and the ever-popular Rumi (d.1273) - 'Attar sat at the pinnacle of the Persian literary renaissance before the Mongol invasion, helping to make poetry into one of Sufism's most powerful attributes.

The medium of book painting also proved crucial for the dissemination of the *Mantiq al-tayr* and its inspired teachings. From Shiraz to Herat, the ateliers of the Timurid (1370–1507) and Safavid (1501–1722) dynasties produced sumptuous illustrated copies of 'Attar's poem as early as the fifteenth century, revealing which tales most inspired artists and readers at that time (Sturkenboom, 2016). Significantly, and maybe

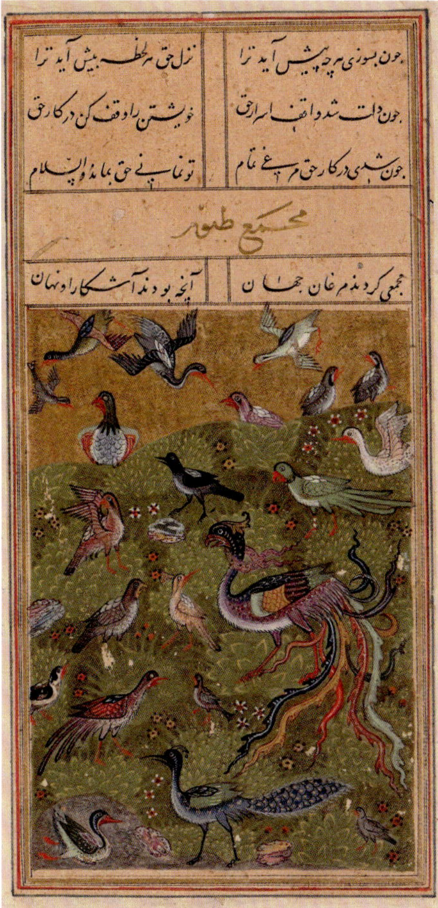

The birds gather together with the hoopoe; *Mantiq al-tayr*, manuscript copied by the scribe Naʿīm al-Dīn of Shiraz, Iran, 1493
Bodleian Libraries, University of Oxford (MS Elliott 246, fol. 25b)

surprisingly, the actual journey of the birds was hardly ever illustrated in these early interpretations. Exceptions appear in two late fifteenth-century copies of the *Mantiq al-tayr* – one in the Bodleian Libraries, Oxford (left) and the other in The Metropolitan Museum of Art, New York. Both capture the dubious voyagers debating how to reach their sovereign (Kamada, 2010; Scollay, 2012). They both also record the individual characteristics of the birds so effectively that even twenty-first century viewers can identify them. Ali Kazim's centrepiece in this exhibition, *Conference of Birds*, is heir to this past mastery, but also offers the flight of the birds its first powerful visual interpretation, masterfully capturing the drive and commitment of the travellers as they take off on their transformative journey.

Deeply influenced by Sufism, and 'Attar in particular, Kazim is a master at reimagining and reinterpreting traditional material and visual culture in a contemporary vein. While scholars debate the details of the poet's life and death, oral traditions abound within the folklore of the Indian subcontinent. Of these, the most repeated legend recounts the meeting with a poor *fakir* (religious ascetic who lives on alms) in 'Attar's famous perfume shop (the word *'attar* meaning 'perfumer' in Persian). The beggar's presence in the opulent shop makes 'Attar uncomfortable and he asks the man to leave. The *fakir* says he has no difficulty with his ragged looking self and undertakes to leave, but not before asking 'Attar how he plans to depart the world with all that he has accumulated. 'Attar retorts that his soul will leave his body in just the same way as the *fakir*'s will. In response, the *fakir* promptly lies down on the ground and his soul departs his body. This encounter leaves a deep impression on 'Attar, who leaves his trade to travel extensively in search of true wisdom.

Kazim's process and practice inspire him to search for connections with the past and find alternative understandings of reality. In every work, including *Conference of Birds*, Kazim seeks ways of understanding the forces that shape and reshape human beings. His oeuvre is underpinned by the idea of a spiritual encounter that is ultimately a discovery and celebration of the beauty and the divine within everyone. Drawn to the traditional practices and history of the subcontinent and its neighbours, Kazim's five-panel watercolour is an interpretation of 'Attar's mystical poem - a life-size representation of a variety of birds as they begin their quest to locate their true leader. Kazim's delicate and meticulously rendered birds symbolise individual souls flying towards the perpetual and collective human desire for ultimate spiritual unity. The panels were displayed unframed in the exhibition, as Kazim did not wish to physically restrict or capture the birds, letting them 'be free'.

Like all of Kazim's works that appear suspended in time, this large watercolour is charged with other vestiges of the past. Beyond its obvious connections to Sufi poetry, it also captures his interest in the refined natural history studies commissioned between 1777 and 1782. These meticulously detailed, life-sized pictures of birds and animals were produced on large sheets of paper by Mughal artists such as Shaikh Zain ud-Din, Bhawani Das and Ram Das. Kazim's five-panel watercolour retains the format and plain ground of such scientific studies, showing great assurance and sensitivity in the birds' elegantly flowing outlines and finely painted plumage and legs. Flying alongside each other, the large flock of different species appear united as they soar upwards in a graceful composition that renders their plumage in subtle and effective greys and black tones. While large in scale, there is an impermanent and fragile quality in the material and medium. This is echoed in his faded monochromatic ruins and self-portraits, also displayed in the exhibition.

Kazim's 2020 *Bird Hunter* series introduces hurdles that the birds must face in their quest - many will not survive. Like 'Attar's poem, Kazim's works suggest a commitment to perseverance and faith. While hunters have no place in 'Attar's narrative, they feature in Kazim's exploration of Sufism and the experience

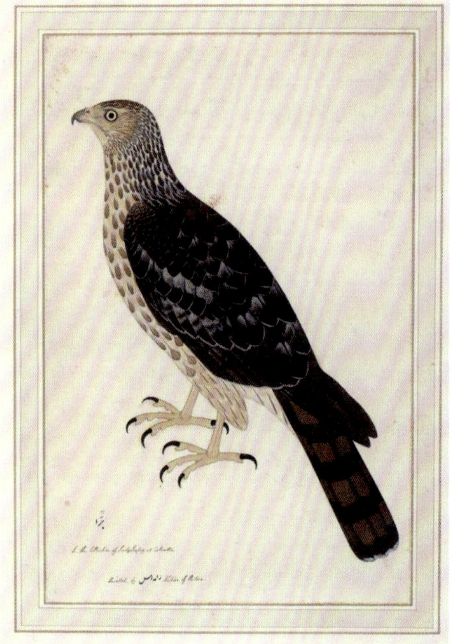

Ram Das, Crested honey buzzard, gouache on paper, 87.4 x 58.9 cm, Kolkata, commissioned by Mary Impey, c.1780
Bodleian Libraries, on long term loan to Ashmolean (LI901.9)

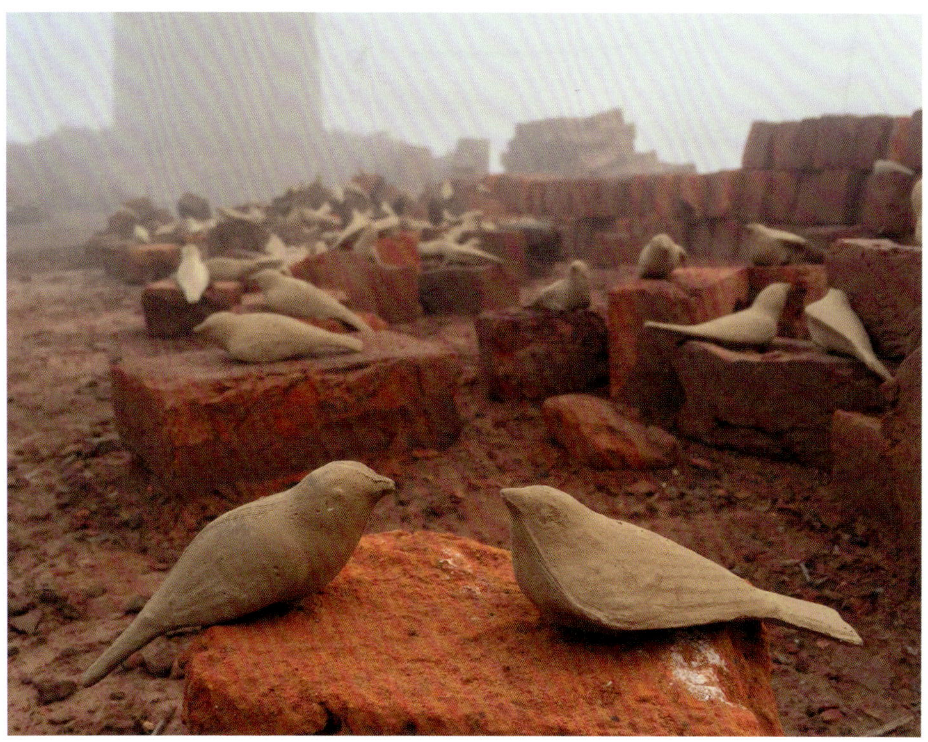

Lahore Biennale, 2020, *Conference of Birds* (detail), installation
©Ali Kazim

beyond the rituals of Islam: the journey towards a personal experience of God and the inner personal aspects of faith. Instead of focusing on the 30 birds that survive the journey, Kazim wonders about those who did not make it; he calls them 'the heroes' that make it possible for others to reach their goal. For a clay installation of *Conference of Birds* at the Lahore Biennale in 2020, Kazim created 3,000 sundried, unfired clay birds. Displayed outside, within the barely standing walls of a ruined building, the clay birds literally dissolved in the rain by the end of the show. (The exhibition includes video footage of the installation) During his 2019 residency Kazim was delighted to find several clay birds, including a *hoopoe*, in the Ashmolean's collection. These birds inspired the installation several months later in Lahore.

Like the work of other contemporary practitioners in the region, Kazim's reinventions of 'Attar's story confirm this tale's timeless value. Furthermore, by reimagining and reanimating the objects held in the Ashmolean Museum, he has ensured that the tale's message remains relevant.

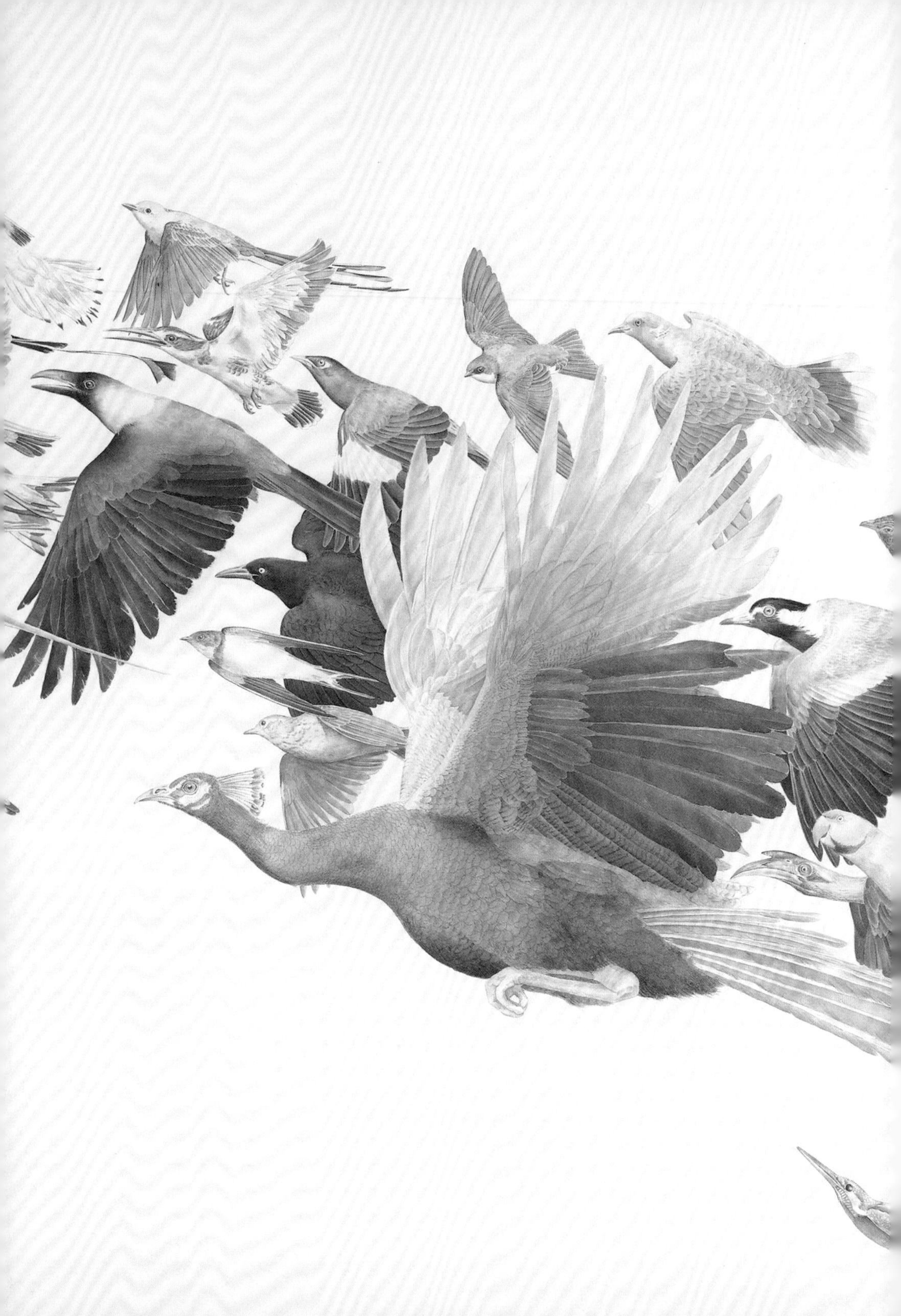

Nishant Kumar

THE CONFERENCE OF THE BIRDS AND PEOPLE IN TROPICAL CITIES

'Science is the art of the soluble'
- Peter Medawar

FOR ECOLOGISTS STUDYING the co-existence of humans and animals, Ali Kazim's body of work resonates remarkably well in addressing the (false) dichotomy of art and science. His symbolic take on Attar's story of Simurgh and *Conference of the Birds* can be examined in the context of urban expansion along the migratory flyways in tropical areas. In tropical countries, long-term co-existence of migratory birds with humans in urban settings often relates to their interactions with anthropogenic resources, shaped by socio-cultural and economic factors. Such dynamic nature-culture relationships have motivated artistic expressions ever since the time of cave paintings. Humans have been interpreting the behaviour and appearance of animals in classifying non-humans - or animals - in folklore, art and scriptures. These works frequently depict animals in their relative association to humans, largely divided along anthropocentric or ecocentric lines.

Ali Kazim, *Conference of Birds, in 5 parts* (detail), 2019, watercolour pigments on paper, 198 x 570 cm
©Ali Kazim, courtesy Jhaveri Contemporary

In many traditional Asian beliefs, a common soul connects all life forms to the one ultimate God form. This belief enables people to be respectful of - and tolerant towards - all wildlife species: they are God's beings within tropical ecosystems. Such social practices and beliefs are a likely precursor to anthropomorphism involving birds. Furthermore, anthropomorphic practices are also reflected in folklore, in the type of animals depicted to express human virtues and philosophical symbolism. As an ecologist looking at Ali Kazim's work, I would interpret the 30 migrating birds broadly on the basis of increasing proximity and tolerance for humans, and how this proximity symbolises the attainment of spiritual awakening, moving from right to left. Ali Kazim's representation of cohesion and collective virtues that form societies is aligned to the latest advances on the study of collective animal behaviours (Couzin, 2009). The latest scientific research on the abilities of migratory birds should dissolve the misconception common in western societies that birds are somehow stupid and inspire the idiom 'bird-brained'.

As they expand through the twenty-first century, tropical cities will impact non-human organisms in shared habitats. The environment of cities - and the amount of food waste available - can shape how and when birds migrate. Conversely, based on how predictable anthropogenic resources become important for wintering birds, human behaviour in different regions support certain populations and/or species, depending on whether they are considered economically or culturally valuable. Cities are also reeling under the pressures of human migration from rural areas. Therefore, as urban destinations for a select set of migratory birds and people, cities in the Global South can be compared to the 'collective' essence of *Qaf*.

This ongoing epoch in earth's geological history, characterised by human domination over ecological systems, is called the Anthropocene. The most worrying aspect of this epoch is the scale of the loss of species, referred to as an ongoing 'sixth mass extinction'. Due to anthropogenic impacts, we are destroying species that avoid urban-systems at about 1000 times the rate of extinction which naturally happens in the background. Human relationships with animals have changed while we transitioned from being hunter-gatherers to agriculturists who practice animal husbandry. These changes include reverse migrations, and massive alterations to migratory connectivity and breeding ecology. Based on their relative tolerance for human-systems, scientists have generally categorised birds as urban avoiders, sub-urban adaptable or urban exploiters.

Human-bird interactions affect the perceptions for birds in cultural landscapes, in mainly three interconnected ways. Firstly, in mutualistic human-bird relationships, e.g., observed in African tribesmen and the greater honey-guide

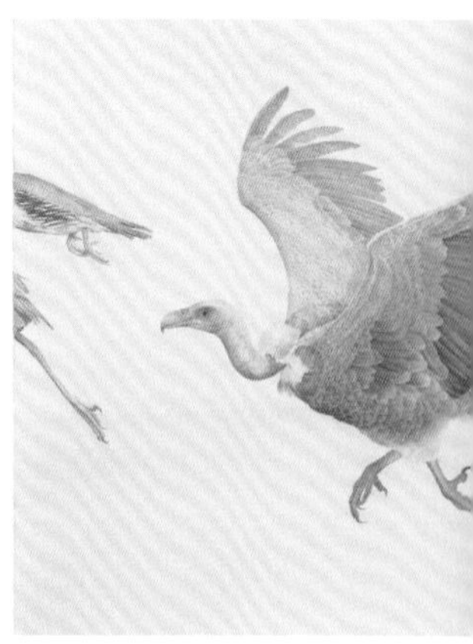

Ali Kazim, *Conference of Birds, in 5 parts* (detail), 2019, watercolour pigments on paper, 198 x 570 cm

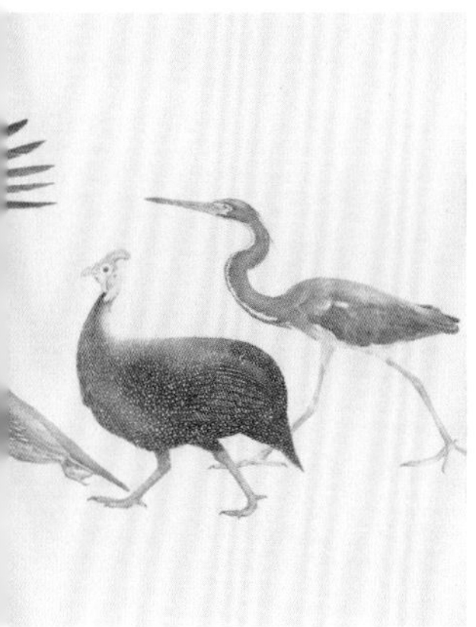

(Spottiswoode et al. 2006). Secondly, via opportunistic scavenging that helps in removal of offal and debris, and prevents infectious zoonotic diseases like rabies (Kumar et al. 2019). And, finally, via cultural services of birds in nature that form and are part of the traditional ecological knowledge.

Simurgh represents an allegorical contest between wilderness and civilisation

In many ways Kazim's depiction of *Conference of Birds* and the mythical Simurgh can help humans understand the scientific concepts of urban ecology, bird migration and urban sustainability. Cities have provided the opportunity for human societies to expand exponentially. They currently house more than 50% of the people on Earth, but occupy only 3% of global land area. It puts cities in perspective for sustainability of ecosystems that are dominated or impacted by human activities. Rapid urbanisation within cities of the Global South poses major developmental questions that concern food security for the growing human populations, and collective health concerns of humans, animals and the environment.

As a species, humans are nowhere near as special as we like to think. Modern scientific understanding of our deleterious impacts on biodiversity reflects the experience of those birds that do not survive the journey – a 'real life Qaf' (Cardinale et al. 2012). Much like what *Conference of the Birds* identified as a reflection of the migratory mixed-flock's collective self, answers for global sustainability will come from identifying and strengthening traditional practices, with modern technological support. Kazim's Simurgh helps us visualise the potential impacts of pollution, unsustainable harvesting of resources and habitat destruction. On the everlasting journey to the *Qaf* of sustainably sharing this planet with non-human organisms, it is important we realise the deleterious human impacts that have caused population declines of *hoopoe* and the regional extinction of vulture-species depicted in Kazim's painting . The modern anthropocentric view makes it more challenging than ever to generate a collective will to conserve what remains of our planet's ecosystems. Scientific understanding of ecology and behaviour in non-humans – combined with traditional cultural practices – will help to address conundrums between modernisation, improving human conditions and protecting diverse, biocultural treasures.

CHRONOLOGY

Compiled by Lauren Winch

1979 Ali Kazim was born in Pattoki, a small village near Lahore, Pakistan.

1982 In an art class for older children in the village school, Kazim (aged just three) drew an image of a mango. The teacher's praise, and comparisons with the older children's works, is an early memory.

1980s Helping to decorate his school for Pakistan Day reinforced his love for art.

1990–94 The origins of Kazim's artistic career can be traced to his apprenticeship as a cinema billboard painter, then painting performers with a traveling circus during the summer after graduating from school. He was also apprenticed to a local potter and furniture wood carver. During his cinema board painting apprenticeship, Kazim first heard about the National College of Arts (NCA).

1995–96 Kazim completed a nursing diploma but remained interested in art, sketching patients and hospital staff while working in Lahore.

1997–98 Kazim encountered an art student making a cityscape and struck up a conversation with him. Under the guidance of this student, Kazim started freehand drawing, mindful that art school entry tests would involve life drawing and an aptitude test.

1998 During what was his first visit to the NCA in Lahore, Kazim took and passed the admission test.

2001 Kazim's work featured for the first time in a group exhibition organised by the Shakir Ali Museum, Lahore.

2002 Kazim achieved his Bachelor in Fine Arts and a Merit Scholarship from the NCA.

2003 Kazim encountered a cast of the Priest-King from Mohenjo-Daro in the Lahore Museum. The original sculpture, in the National Museum of Pakistan in Karachi, was made c.2600–1900 BC. The work is probably the earliest surviving example of a human portrait from the region, and inspired the themes of time, memory and bygone civilisations central to Kazim's work.

His placement with the International Artist Camp (George Keyt Foundation) in Sri Lanka marked the first of many artists' residencies Kazim would undertake across the world. He also exhibited in the

Sri Lankan city of Colombo, at the Lionel Wendt Centre for the Arts.

2004 Paradise Road in Colombo, Sri Lanka, and the Zahoor ul Akhlaq Art Gallery in the NCA, Lahore, featured Kazim's first solo exhibitions. He also completed an artist residency with the Vasl Residency (Triangle Arts Trust) in Karachi, Pakistan.

2005 Kazim travelled to the United Kingdom on the ROSL (Royal Over-Seas League) Travel Scholarship: Residency at Hospitalfield, Arbroath, Scotland. He exhibited jointly at the Scope Art Fair in London, and the 9th National Exhibition of Visual Arts in Lahore.

2006 Kazim's solo exhibition *Sacred Souls, Secret Lives* toured between Green Cardamom, London, Ethan Cohen gallery, New York and Alhamra Art Gallery in Lahore. Group shows this year included the 12th Asian Art Biennale, Bangladesh, *Curious Ties* at The Lab Gallery in New York, and the ROSL scholars group show, Jerwood Space, London.

Both the Victoria and Albert Museum and The Metropolitan Museum of Art added works by Kazim to their collections, and he received the Young Painter Award from the Lahore Arts Council. Kazim's works were acquired by Devi Art Foundation.

2007 Cartwright Hall Art Gallery in Bradford, displayed a survey show exploring Kazim's artistic methods . He exhibited in a solo show at the VM Art Gallery in Karachi, and a group show titled *Inaugural Exhibition* at the National Art Gallery in Islamabad. The Queensland Art Gallery of Modern Art (QAGOMA) in Brisbane, Australia, acquired works by Kazim.

2008 Kazim showed his work at a solo exhibition in Gallery Espace in New Delhi, as well as group shows at the Alhamra Art Gallery in Lahore (*Nocturnal Songs*), at the 13th Asian Art Biennale, Bangladesh and at East-West Center Gallery in Honolulu, Hawaii. Kazim's portraits were acquired by the QAGOMA.

2009 Kazim joined the Slade School of Fine Art in London. The solo exhibition *Rider* appeared at Green Cardamon in London, and Rohtas 2 Gallery in Lahore. Speelhuislaan 171 in Breda, Netherlands, included Kazim in their show *Oog In Oog*. The Burger Collection acquired Kazim's works.

2010 Kazim returned to London's Green Cardamon with the group exhibition *Drawn from Life: Drawing Form*, while also exhibiting in Beyond the Page at the Pacific Asia Museum in Pasadena, USA. The British Museum acquired Kazim's *Peacock Boy*.

2011 Ali Kazim earned an MFA from the Slade in London. While studying, he explored Indus and Mesopotamian terracotta held by museums in London.

Kazim shared a studio space in Bow Arts, East London with two other graduates from the Royal Academy of Arts and Royal College of Art. All three won the Land Securities Studio Award for their degree shows. The same year Kazim was also a finalist for the Catlin Art Prize, and won the Melville Nettleship Prize for Figural Composition.

He exhibited at Abbot Hall, Kendal, in the touring exhibition, *Drawn from Life*. Hong Kong creative cities acquired a work by Kazim. Meanwhile, on his return to Pakistan, he began regularly visiting ruins and archaeological sites.

2012 Green Cardamon displays solo exhibition by Kazim. He also displayed at two group exhibitions in London: Creative Cities Collection at the Barbican, and Catlin Art Prize Exhibition, Londonewcastle Project Space. The British Museum acquired a life size full figure self-portrait. In New York, Kazim featured in the ArtGate Gallery's drawing show *Chosen*. In the same year he joined the NCA as a visiting faculty member.

2013 Kazim began working with Jhaveri Contemporary, featuring in a solo exhibition in Mumbai, India. His art also featured in a trio of group shows across London: *Heritage Reinvented* at the Tryon St Gallery, *Be a Man!* at the Sumarria Lunn Gallery, and Portraits at the Selma Feriani Gallery. Kazim's work was included in an exhibition that brought together 250 objects from the British Museum at the Bundeskunsthalle in Bonn, Germany. The exhibition was titled *Treasures of the World's Cultures - The Great Collections: The British Museum*.

2014 Kazim completed a residency at The Art House in Wakefield, England. Group exhibitions this year included the touring of *Portraits* to the Selma Feriani Gallery in Tunisia, *Ethereal* at the Leila Heller Gallery in New York, and *The Importance of Staying Quiet* at the Yallay Gallery in Hong Kong. Pacific Asia Museum in Pasadena acquired Kazim's work.

2015 Kazim appeared in a group exhibition organised by Jhaveri Contemporary at Art Dubai. His art also showcased at the exhibitions *Human Image: Masterpieces of figurative art from the British Museum* at Seoul Arts Center, South Korea, and *Dust* at the Ujazdowski Castle Centre for Contemporary Art in Poland.

2016 Rohatas 2 Gallery, Lahore curated two solo exhibitions of Kazim's work: Ali Kazim: *Untitled* and *Of Darkness and Light*. Jhaveri Contemporary showcased Kazim's Ruins series at Asian Art in London.

This year Kazim also appeared in the group shows *Universal/Personal* at the Hinterland Galerie in Vienna, and *The Missing One*, which toured between the Office for Contemporary Art Norway in Oslo, and Dhaka Art Summit in Bangladesh. Kiran Nadar Museum of Art acquired works by Kazim.

2017 Kazim was appointed Assistant Professor at the NCA, Lahore. At the Karachi Biennale, Pakistan, he won the Mahvash & Jahangir Siddiqui Foundation Juried Art Prize. The same year, his work was displayed in the Drawing Biennial at the Drawing Room in London. Other group exhibitions included *Grisaille* at Leila Heller Gallery, New York, and *What Is Seen And Not Seen With And Without Seeing*, at Gandhara-art Space, Karachi.

2018 Kazim worked once again with Jhaveri Contemporary, displaying his work at Art Basel Hong Kong: Discoveries. Here he was a finalist for the BMW Art Journey award. He also featured in the Lahore Biennale and the 9th Asia Pacific Triennial of Contemporary Art (APT 9) at

QAGOMA, Australia. QAGOMA acquired a large-scale landscape from the ruins series, and drawings from the cloud series as well as the storm series.

2019 Continuing his work with Jhaveri Contemporary, Kazim shared a solo exhibition of his work at Abu Dhabi, and displayed in group shows at the Indian Art Fair in New Delhi and the Frieze in New York. He also appeared at the Karachi Biennale, COMO Museum of Art in Lahore, and in the Drawing Biennial at the Drawing Room in London.

University of Oxford's Classical Art Research Centre, in collaboration with the Ashmolean Museum of Art and Archaeology, invited Kazim to be Artist-in-Residence on the Gandhara Connections research project. Kazim was inspired by the Museum's Indus, Gandharan, Mughal, Rajput, and Company School objects. Reflecting on these works, he reimagined new works for a future show.

2020 Kazim exhibited his work at another major Biennale in Pakistan, this time at Lahore. Grosvenor Gallery in London presented his art in the group exhibition, *Form & Figure: Bodies of Art.*

2021 Group shows included the Drawing Biennial at the Drawing Room in London, and in Islamabad, Pakistan.

2022 Kazim returned to the Ashmolean Museum for a solo exhibition, *Ali Kazim: Suspended in Time*, which presented his work together with objects from the Museum's collection that inspired Kazim during his residency in 2019.

CONTRIBUTORS

Dr Faisal Devji is Professor of Indian History at the University of Oxford, and Fellow of St Antony's College, Oxford. He is interested in the intellectual history and political thought of modern South Asia, as well as in the emergence of Islam as a global category. His recent work deals with efforts to think beyond the nation-state and the inheritance of anarchism in the post-colonial world.

Sir Tim Hitchens KCVO CMG is President of Wolfson College, Oxford. He came to Wolfson in 2018 after 35 years in the British Diplomatic Service. His last overseas posting was as British Ambassador to Tokyo. Before that he was Africa Director. His postings took him to Pakistan, Afghanistan, France and Japan. For four years he was also Assistant Private Secretary to the Queen.

Dr Nishant Kumar is Visiting Fellow in Ethno-ornithology at the University of Oxford, and a Postdoctoral Researcher in the Wildlife Institute of India, Dehradun. He is interested in evolutionary ecology and has worked on vulture conservation advocacy, monitoring of tigers and their prey, and the annual migration of Black-eared kites *Milvus migrans lineatus*. He is interested in the socio-economic impacts of scavenging ecosystem services, and how their biocultural links are vital for a sustainable urban future in South Asia.

Dr Mallica Kumbera Landrus is Keeper (Head) of the Department of Eastern Art. Her curatorial responsibilities are in the area of Indian, Himalayan and Southeast Asian art at the Ashmolean Museum. She is Associate Professor of the History of Indian Art at the University of Oxford, and a Fellow of St Cross College, Oxford. Her research interests focus on the Indian subcontinent, particularly with regard to the intersection of art, architecture, religion, politics and socio-economics.

Dr Francesca Leoni is Assistant Keeper and Curator of Islamic Art at the Ashmolean Museum, University of Oxford. She specialises in the Islamic Middle East, with a focus on the Persian-speaking world. Her research looks at objects as points of departure to pursue larger questions and explore the broader cultural landscapes that produced and consumed them. While she works on a range of media, her primary areas of expertise are illustrated and illuminated manuscripts and metalwork.

Dr Chaitanya Sambrani is Associate Professor at the Centre for Art History and Art Theory and Convenor of Higher Degrees by Research at the School of Art and Design, Australian National University. His research and teaching interests lie in modern and contemporary art in Asia, especially in relation to the politics of tradition, nationhood and belonging.

Dr Peter Stewart is Director of the Classical Art Research Centre, Professor of Ancient Art at the University of Oxford, and Fellow of Wolfson College, Oxford. His research interests lie in the field of ancient sculpture, including Roman provincial art. He also works on connections between classical art and the artistic traditions of Asia, especially the ancient Buddhist sculpture of Gandhara in what is now northern Pakistan.

Dr Emilia Terracciano is Lecturer in Modern Art History at the University of Manchester. Her research interests lie in modern and contemporary art, with a focus on the global south. She is currently working on a monograph about art, nature and future events in the global south. She frequently collaborates with artists, curators and gallerists in the UK, India and Pakistan, and writes for the art press.

Lauren Winch is a History of Art student in her final year at Worcester College, Oxford. Between 2020 and 2021 she undertook a student placement in the Department of Eastern Art at the Ashmolean Museum. The placement has provided her with valuable work experience, while also developing transferable skills for the future.

REFERENCES

Attar, F., Translated by Davis, D. and Darbandi, A. (1984) *The Conference of the Birds*. Harmondsworth and New York: Penguin Books.

Cardinale, B. J. et al. (2012) 'Biodiversity loss and its impact on humanity', *Nature*, 486 (7401), pp. 59–67.

Couzin, I. (2009) 'Collective cognition in animal groups', *Trends in Cognitive Sciences*, 13 (1), pp. 36–43.

Lewisohn, L. (ed.) (1999) *The Heritage of Sufism*. Oxford and Boston: Oneworld.

Scollay, S. (2012) *Love and Devotion: From Persia and Beyond*. Oxford: Bodleian Library.

Sturkenboom, I. (2016) *The Imagery of the Mantiq al-Tayr: A Fifteenth-Century History of Illustrated Manuscripts incorporating 'Attar's Conference of the Birds.* PhD dissertation, Bamberg University.

Kamada, Y. (2010) 'A Taste for Intricacy: An Illustrated Manuscript of Mantiq al-Tayr in the Metropolitan Museum of Art', *Orient*, 45, pp.129–75

Kumar, N et al. (2019) 'Urban waste and the human-animal interface in Delhi', *Economic and Political Weekly*, 54 (47), pp. 42–47.

Spottiswoode, C. et al. (2016) 'Reciprocal signaling in honeyguide-human mutualism', *Science*, 353 (6297), pp. 387–389.

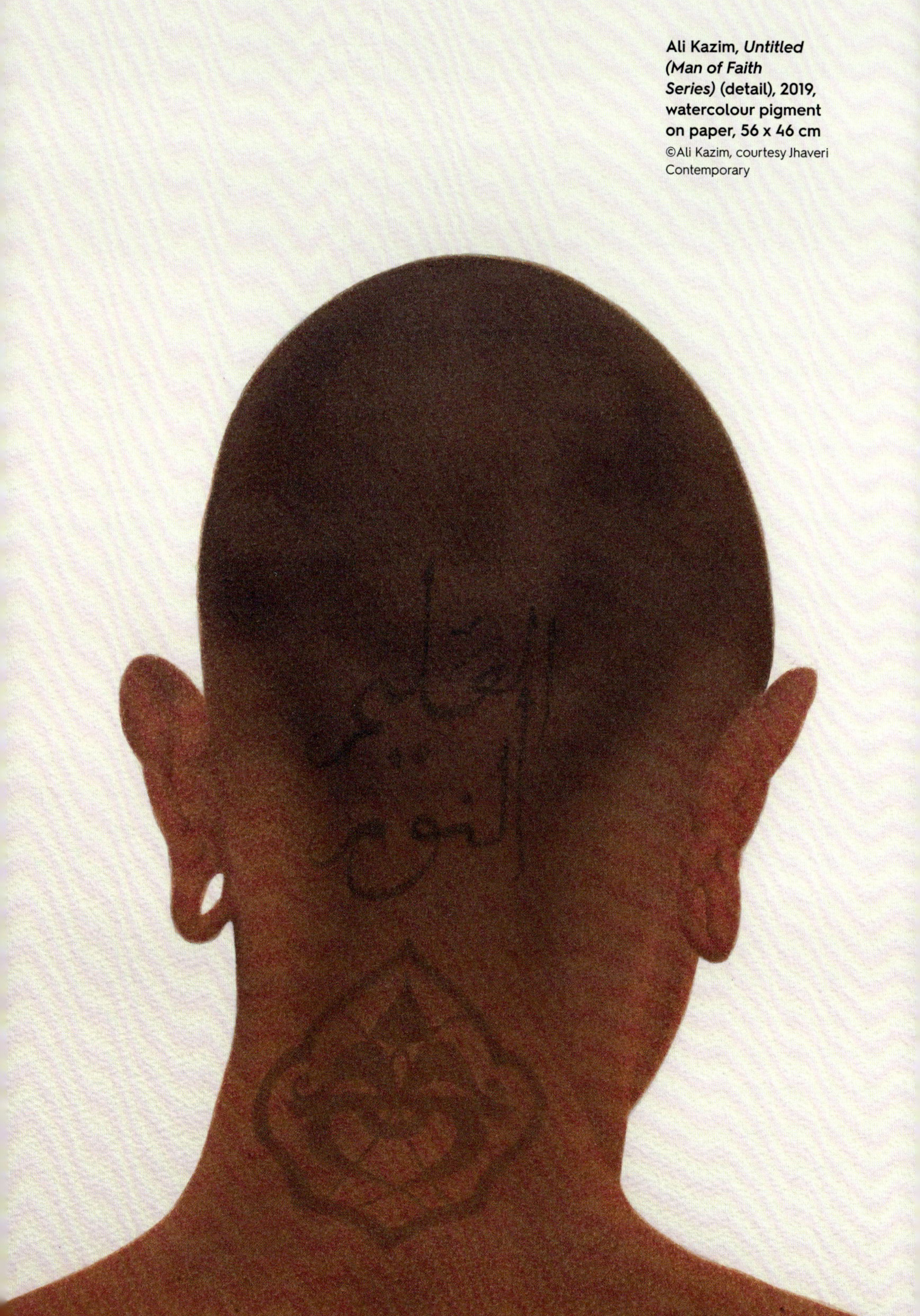

Ali Kazim, *Untitled (Man of Faith Series)* (detail), 2019, watercolour pigment on paper, 56 x 46 cm

©Ali Kazim, courtesy Jhaveri Contemporary

Ali Kazim. Suspended in Time
Ashmolean Museum, from 7 Feb to 26 June 2022

Mallica Kumbera Landrus, Tim Hitchens, Faisal Devji, Emilia Terracciano, Peter Stewart, Chaitanya Sambrani, Francesca Leoni, Nishant Kumar and Lauren Winch have asserted their moral rights to be identified as the authors of this work.

British Library Cataloguing in Publications Data

A catalogue record for this book is available from the British Library

ISBN: 978-1-910807-51-4

Catalogue designed by Ocky Murray

Printed and bound in the UK by Gomer Press

For further details of Ashmolean titles please visit:
www.ashmolean.org/shop

MIX
Paper from responsible sources
FSC® C114687

This catalogue publication is supported by the Elie Khouri Art Foundation.

Image credits:
©Ali Kazim, Courtesy Jhaveri Contemporary

Exhibition supported by:
Kamini and Vindi Banga Family Trust
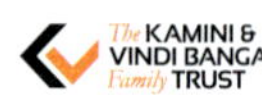

Tia Fine Art Limited
Mr Ben Brown
Mrs Rosamond Brown
ZVM Rangoonwala Foundation
Tarun and Tarana Sawhney
Tarika and Zafar Ahmadullah
Charles Wallace Pakistan Trust
And those who wish to remain anonymous.

We thank the artist, Taimur Hassan, Tarika and Zafar Ahmadullah, Sanda Lwin and Farhad Karim, and Jhaveri Contemporary for their generosity and support with loans.

JHAVERI CONTEMPORARY

(title page) Ali Kazim, *Untitled (Mara's Army)* (detail), 2020, watercolour pigment on paper, 114 x 79 cm
©Ali Kazim, courtesy Jhaveri Contemporary

(p.4) Ali Kazim, *Untitled (Votive Objects)* (detail), 2020, clay, various dimensions
©Ali Kazim, courtesy Jhaveri Contemporary

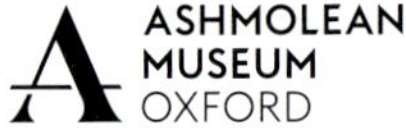

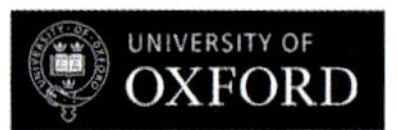